RYA Pass:

C000245552

I ₊

Illustrations by Andrew Simpson

© Peter Chennell 2011
First Published 2011
Reprinted November 2013, March 2016,
June 2017, January 2018, April 2019,
March 2020, January 2021, April 2022,
September 2023

The Royal Yachting Association
RYA House, Ensign Way, Hamble,
Southampton SO31 4YA
Tel: 02380 604 100
Web: www.rya.org.uk

We welcome feedback on our publications
at publications@rya.org.uk

You can check content updates for
RYA publications at
www.rya.org.uk/go/bookschangelog

ISBN: 978-1-905104840
RYA Order Code: G69

Technical Editor: Andrew Simpson
Cover Design: Pete Galvin
Typesetting and Design: KJS
Proofreading and indexing: Alan Thatcher
Printed in the UK
Photo credits: Peter Chennell, Alan Butcher, Andark Diving,
Andrew Simpson

FOREWORD

One of the fabulous things about playing about on boats is the feeling of freedom that comes with it. With very few 'road signs' and even fewer marked lanes to show you where you should go, there's a real feeling of being master of your own destiny.

However all experienced boaters will know that the hazards are all there – they are just deceptively concealed beneath the surface.

It's just good sense to prepare thoroughly before setting off on any passage. Researching and planning difficult port entrances and tricky hazards from the comfort of your own living room before setting off is so much easier than doing it when sitting below at the chart table in a building seaway as you approach an unfamiliar port in the dark.

Planning only needs to be as complicated as the passage requires. A two mile ride in a RIB in familiar waters will require significantly less attention than a 100 mile passage on a sailing vessel bound for somewhere you have never been before. This book will assist you greatly in judging just how much passage planning is required for every situation.

Once you have read this book I am sure you will agree that the safety of yourself, your family and friends and, of course, your boat really does justify a small investment in time and effort to plan your passage before you actually depart.

Safe boating.

Richard Falk
RYA Director of Training & Qualifications

INTRODUCTION

You've run out of coffee, and the local shop is a short walk away. You look at the weather, decide you need a coat, check you've got your wallet, and leave, remembering to pocket the front door key. You have to cross a busy road, and elect to cross it in one, rather than use the pedestrian crossing a few hundred metres further along. You check your watch, and wonder if the shop will still be open, but are unconcerned since there's a garage a little further on, which will have the basics.

When you get to the shop, in effect you will have completed a passage and, prior to it, done some passage planning, albeit subconsciously. You might have undertaken a similar thought process if you had been setting out on a longer journey by car, except your considerations might have been more concerned with other issues.

When this, the most basic of all planning exercises is applied to a journey at sea, it acquires the magic of a black art: it becomes passage planning. It need not be complicated, but an element is required for even the simplest, and shortest of journeys.

This book has relevance to all who take their recreation afloat. It won't teach the basic skills of boat handling, navigation, nor the other aspects of seamanship, but much will be relevant to all levels of experience, and aspirations. It's a book to be referred to at home (probably where most passage planning is done). In fact this is probably the one book that could be left at home rather than taken on board. It will have done its job if you can set off confident that you'll have taken all factors into consideration.

The planning guidelines that follow will cover all sorts of passages: in sheltered waters, along a coast, in open waters, or even trans-ocean adventures. Whatever type of boat you have and whatever purpose takes you to sea there are elements that will have real appropriateness to you.

There are no rules to be found in the following chapters. Take from them what applies to you, develop your own lists, aides memoire, and routines, or use the examples provided.

Make passage planning routine.

CONTENTS

The marina at St Peter Port

1 GETTING DOWN TO BASICS

Let's look at an example

Roy and Jean had chartered a sailing boat for two weeks, and were returning to Lymington from a holiday in the West Country. They arrived in Weymouth late, knowing that their final leg would take them home. Roy studied the tidal atlases and decided they needed a very early start to take advantage of the favourable tides. The weather forecast was south-west F4–5 increasing F6–7 later.

In the event, they had a rollicking sail home to the Solent, though the wind increased much earlier than forecast, veering to west. Since the wind was with the tide, they were sailing free. The boat coped well, bringing a very satisfactory end to an excellent holiday.

Although Roy had made this passage before he had still checked the tide times and heights at Poole, a port on the way where they could seek shelter if the weather deteriorated.

 So what were the things Roy did to make the day go so well?

- In the first instance he needed to 'work' the strong tidal streams in that area to his advantage. There's a critical point along the route, at St Albans Head, where the tides run fiercely, and large overfalls can arise in some conditions. He saw that the streams are relatively slack in Weymouth Bay, but flow strongly east/west thereafter
- Roy didn't want to be punching the tide

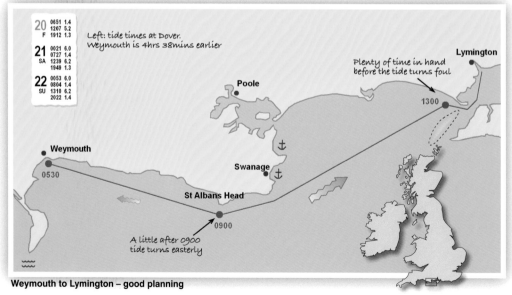

20 F
0651 1.4
1207 5.2
1912 1.3

21 SA
0021 6.0
0727 1.4
1239 6.2
1949 1.3

22 SU
0053 6.0
0804 1.4
1310 6.2
2022 1.4

Left: tide times at Dover.
Weymouth is 4hrs 38mins earlier

Lymington

Plenty of time in hand before the tide turns foul

1300

Poole

Weymouth

0530

Swanage

St Albans Head

0900

A little after 0900 tide turns easterly

Weymouth to Lymington – good planning

all the way, and certainly needed to have a fair tide to get through Hurst Narrows – about 20nm to the east of St Albans Head, no more than a four hour leg, given a fair tide and following wind. He also knew that at that time there would be no overfalls, so he could take the more direct, inshore route, arriving at Lymington in the dying moments of his favourable tide. As a precaution, he noted the tide times for Poole in case the weather deteriorated and they were obliged to seek shelter.

■ Assessing all the various factors, he decided that they should be rounding St Albans Head shortly after the time the tide turned to flood eastwards at that point. But first, of course, they would have to fight the weaker adverse tide to get there. Working backwards from St Albans Head it was clear that they needed to be away from Weymouth by 0600.

How it might have gone wrong

In a parallel universe Roy and Jean had chartered a boat for two weeks, and were returning to Lymington from a holiday in the West Country. They arrived in Weymouth late, knowing that the final leg would take them home. Well…

■ They slept in, missing the weather forecast. After a leisurely breakfast in a local café, they eventually got under way around noon.

■ The wind by now was blowing a good F6 from the west and, when they got to St Albans Head, they found the combination of wind over tide had kicked up a very uncomfortable sea, which slowed them down considerably. About this time Jean felt the first uneasy signs of seasickness.

■ With no choice but to carry on they arrived at the Needles to discover that the sea had built still further. Enormous, in fact.

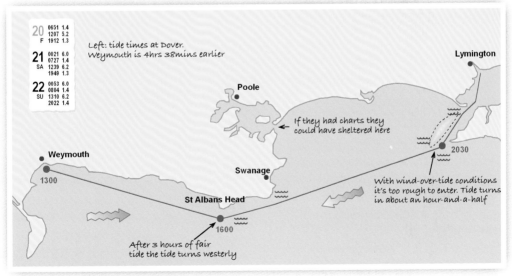

Weymouth to Lymington – bad planning

- By now Jean was making her anxiety known, and became increasingly upset as Roy explained that they had no choice but to stick it out until the tide turned so that they could have a more comfortable ride down the Needles Channel. Although Roy had charts to cover the passage he had no large scale charts of Poole and its approaches, and also wasn't aware of the alternative northerly route around the Shingles Bank to the west of the Isle of Wight. What was worse was that he was on a lee shore wherever he looked. When they finally arrived cold, exhausted, and thoroughly dispirited, this dreadful journey had rather taken the shine out of what had been a pleasant holiday.

What went right, what went wrong?

The difference between these two voyages is obvious. With a little thought and planning the unpleasant journey could easily have been made bearable. They could have stopped temporarily in Studland Bay. They also could have had a more comfortable ride by going close to Hurst. Without an awareness of the tides, without an appraisal of the alternatives, and without carrying the necessary charts and references, what should have been a simple journey turned out to be one they would rather forget.

The difference between these two voyages was planning – passage planning. It can make or break a good day out, a weekend, a holiday, or life's great adventure. It can make boating more comfortable, more fun, less frightening, and gets you to where you want to be safely. It avoids rows, it is less stressful, and is satisfying. It makes boating more fun.

SOLAS V

At this point, and before we move on, it must be stated that passage planning is more than just the practice of good seamanship. It's an obligation for all seafarers by international agreement.

The acronym 'SOLAS' stands for the International Convention for the Safety Of Life At Sea. Most of these rules and regulations apply only to large commercial ships, but parts of chapter V (hence SOLAS V) apply to small privately owned pleasure craft – everywhere. This means that everybody who goes to sea in a vessel of some sort is bound to it by law.

The section of SOLAS V that is so important is regulation V/34, "Safe navigation and avoidance of dangerous situations". The text

Regulation V/34

Regulation V/34 'Safe Navigation and avoidance of dangerous situations', is a new regulation. It concerns prior-planning for your boating trip, more commonly known as voyage or passage planning. Voyage planning is basically common sense. As a pleasure boat user, you should particularly take into account the following points when planning a boating trip:

- **Weather:** before you go boating, check the weather forecast and get regular updates if you are planning to be out for any length of time.
- **Tides:** check the tidal predictions for your trip and ensure that they fit with what you are planning to do.
- **Limitations of the vessel:** consider whether

in the panel below is abstracted from the Maritime and Coastguard Agency's leaflet MCA/098. This is available via www.dft.gov.uk/mca.

What it boils down to do for us recreational mariners is that we are obliged to make a passage plan containing a useful level of information. Most importantly of all, there's a requirement to be able to show that you have indeed produced the plan. So if your intended passage is to go out of the harbour along the coast for a mile or two, drop anchor in a secluded bay, have a picnic lunch, maybe some swimming and then return, you need to have something to demonstrate you have considered the factors that may influence your journey – not necessarily in writing.

So what would be acceptable voyage planning, in accordance with SOLAS, for a proposed journey? It could be as rudimentary as scribbled notes on a scrap of paper, but, better still, would be a small index card or even a wipe-clean waterproof page. On it there should be a summary of the weather forecast, and a note of high tide (and maybe tidal flow, notes on any navigational dangers, courses and maybe some waypoints). Also there should be a note of an alternative port of refuge or anchorage if there is one. It's about proving that you have complied with the spirit of the law – not the specifics of every detail.

Naturally, simple journeys require simple notes, while the longer ones will need proportionately more input and are therefore proportionately more difficult to produce. At the end of the day it's all down to common sense. There is no legal requirement to write one.

So what is passage planning? How is it done? What are the 'tricks of the trade', where are they applied and when should they be used?

your boat is up to the proposed trip and that you have sufficient safety equipment and stores with you.

- **Crew:** *take into account the experience and physical ability of your crew. Crews suffering from cold, tiredness and seasickness won't be able to do their job properly and could even result in an overburdened skipper.*

- **Navigational dangers:** *make sure you are familiar with any navigational dangers you may encounter during your boating trip. This generally means checking an up to date chart and a current pilot book or almanac.*

- **Contingency plan:** *always have a contingency plan should anything go wrong. Before you go, consider bolt holes and places where you can take refuge should conditions deteriorate or if you suffer an incident or injury. Bear in mind that your GPS set is vulnerable and could fail at the most inconvenient time. It is sensible and good practice to make sure you are not over-reliant on your GPS set and that you can navigate yourself to safety without it should it fail you.*

- **Information ashore:** *make sure that someone ashore knows your plans and knows what to do should they become concerned for your well being. The RYA Safetrx app (Safetrx has replaced the Coastguard Voluntary Safety Identification Scheme (CG66)) is also free and easy to use. The scheme aims to help the Coastguard to help you quickly should you get into trouble while boating. It could save your life.*

2 THE ESSENTIAL FIRST STEPS

Almost every journey needs a plan – some of which might be formed in the subconscious. This will include:

- An objective – a reason for doing it
- Constraints which might limit one's options
- Awareness of hazards that might need to be avoided
- Aids which could contribute to an effective journey by avoiding difficulties or by making the journey easier
- Finally, a route. How this route is chosen depends very much on the preceding four elements of the plan. And there may, of course, be alternatives.

Let's take those steps one at a time.

Appraise the undertaking

So, every journey needs to have an objective, no matter how trivial. Getting from one port to another, going round the bay, visiting a favourite anchorage or perhaps to a favourite fishing or diving spot – they are all reasons for undertaking a passage. And there's no reason why you shouldn't have conditional objectives – 'cross the Channel to Cherbourg, but only if the wind is in the west,' for instance.

This articulation of the objective is the first step in passage planning. Only once this objective is identified can you determine the criteria under which you are prepared to make your journey. Limiting criteria might include: weather, sea state, time available, size or

Every passage plan ends in a destination – some as nice as this

condition of the boat, and views of the family or crew etc. Much can depend on weather forecasts. For example, a young family might not care for an extended beat to windward, but would be content if the journey were off the wind.

The passage plan shape and format becomes much more evident once you establish the circumstances under which you are ready to go. It's much easier to plan many of the various aspects of your journey in advance. Try not to regard this as a scientific

process. It's not – though it involves some of the discipline of science. It is merely being clear in one's mind about the enjoyment you are setting out to experience.

Once the objective is articulated, the next step is an appraisal of the type of journey you're planning and the consideration of all the factors that are likely to influence on what you're setting out to do. These factors, most of them simple in nature, need determining and the process is one of observation, analysis and evaluation.

Passage planning basics

The longer and more complicated the passage, the more thought you must spend on its planning. Set aside plenty of time for the task, and allot yourself enough space to spread the various bits of reference material about.

Start by assembling the bits and pieces you will need. Depending upon the location and the nature of your plans, these will probably include:

- Charts of the area to an appropriate scale. A short passage might call for a single chart; a longer passage several.
- Navigational almanac.
- Pilot books or guides.
- Tidal stream atlas.
- Pencil (2B is ideal), eraser and sharpener.
- Notepad.
- Dividers.
- Breton plotter/parallel rulers/rolling ruler.
- Somewhere to spread it all out.

As for skills, you must be confident that your level of expertise is appropriate to the task. At the very minimum you should be capable of basic plotting. The likelihood is that you will have completed some form of RYA training but, if not, the RYA Navigation Handbook would be a very good way to start.

Make sure any previous pencil marks are erased from your chart and arrange it so that you can see the whole of the intended passage. Have a good look at it and assess the undertaking. Roughly measure out the distances and ask yourself fundamental questions. Is the journey do-able? If you want to go from say Place A to Port B, assess how far it is, and how long will it take. Think about it a bit more. If you're in a yacht and contemplating a 60 mile passage, are you content with 12 or more hours on board?

Absorb the coastline. Look at headlands and see if there are any associated patches of rough water. Are there any areas of shallows in the area covered by the line joining A to B? If you are contemplating an open water passage, what about shipping movements?

Don't be afraid to scribble notes on the chart, no matter how trivial. That's what it's for!

If your destination is unfamiliar to you, look it up in the almanac or the pilot guide. You may be instantly deterred. It may have hazardous approaches, it may be very tidal, or perhaps be one of those places where a leisure boat just doesn't feel welcome amongst all the commercial freight and fishing vessels.

Bear in mind that a challenging port is better approached after a short passage rather than an extended one when people are tired and getting careless. A common mistake is to try and cram too much into a limited time frame. Don't be too ambitious.

Think about other sources of information, such as the internet. Or you may know someone who is familiar with the area. A quick phone call or email could yield all sorts of useful insights.

Once you have got the 'feel' of the voyage, you will feel able to move on to the next step.

More detailed planning

When you get down to detailed planning it divides broadly into two groups: firstly, what you might label 'geographic' and, secondly, considerations which you might label 'practical' – with a possibility even of a third group called 'social'.

For many, the detailed planning of a journey is both fun and exciting, full of pleasurable anticipation. Sometimes it can be done during the winter, foretelling the pleasures of summer, or it might be done in the days before a proposed passage, or even at the point of departure. Different passages need different amounts of input, with the simplest needing very little but the basics.

Some of the key factors might need a bit of thought, perhaps some investigation or even research. It doesn't all have to be done at once – for example some early planning might be conversations with family or friends about what the summer may bring, with a later stage being a more detailed consideration of what is involved, leading to a final commitment on the day of departure.

The journey

In most cases the journey itself is evident. We're usually pretty clear about where we want to go. However, it might be worth a moment just to pause and confirm that the destination we think is ideal is actually the right choice. For instance, many sailors make the passage westwards across Lyme Bay from Poole or further east. Lyme Bay is quite a long passage (every bit as far as Poole to Cherbourg) and the temptation is to aim for the first point of arrival, which is Brixham. However Dartmouth isn't much further on. Another consideration is to position the boat in order to make the next leg as easy as possible. When crossing

the Channel bound for South Brittany many people choose to make the passage through the Chenal du Four at the end of the cross-Channel leg, taking a rest day in Camaret. It's rare for people to go into Brest, particularly as it's a little further, but there's much to recommend it.

Timing

Why? At the risk of being pedantic, it might be worth asking why you want to make this particular passage. Sometimes we get stuck in a groove and do things automatically, which often denies us the opportunity to visit new places. Another reason in support of the 'why?' question is to consider what the limitations of you, your boat, and your crew are. In the eagerness to get away we often fail to take account of the requirements of others. Maybe your partner and possibly children don't want to spend the first day on a windward thrash of 18 hours, preferring instead a short hop just to get into the routine of shipboard life. If your answer is 'I've got to' you're guilty of one of the worst contributors to boat misery. It forces the crew into weather that is very stressful, and places everyone in positions where they're likely to make mistakes. It may be that you have to be back at the office on Monday, or will miss two ports of your planned cruise but, in the grand scheme of things, these are less important than the safety of yourself, your boat, and the people with whom you share it. Countless incidents at sea happened because people have set out on journeys that are inappropriate at the time. Don't be lured into this process. It rarely ends in joy.

Type of passage

At this point it's appropriate to dwell on the type of passage being undertaken. I have made the point that passage planning has themes common to all types of voyage, and generally they don't overlap. So, if your intended journey is a short cruise to a port only a handful of miles away then, almost by definition, you are unable to do little more than check the weather, the tides and the readiness to go to sea. Alternative ports probably don't exist, and a quick glance at the chart will determine whether there are any hazards; some bearings and courses may need to be noted and that's it. Compare this with how much detail would be needed to go into an open water passage.

Acceptability

Another point concerns the level of acceptability either to you or to others. It's possible to make the mistake of assuming that everyone will have fun. The good skipper will make sure that they have taken the strengths and weaknesses of their companions into account. It might help, therefore, to have alternative passages in mind. Perhaps a cross-Channel trip will only go ahead if the weather forecast indicates a favourable wind. A motorboat might similarly consider sea state. Divers might find a passage timing inappropriate if they don't get to their dive site within a certain tidal window. Whatever the

> **TIP** The complexity of the passage you are undertaking will determine the level of input and research needed.

acceptability level, it's an important issue at this early part of passage planning, as it stops us setting unacceptable goals.

Start with a picture

The very first thing you need to do is to have a visual picture of your passage. In many cases this will involve spreading out a chart and marking the intended route on it in soft pencil (2B is ideal). This will give you a broad picture of your undertaking and is worthwhile even in familiar territory. Indicate areas – not necessarily on the route – which might be a hazard. Also mark any tidal gates, headlands, locks, and drying areas which may have critical timings. Electronic chartplotters and the like typically allow annotations to be made on their screens.

The next step is to begin to marry the broad picture with some of the more critical events along the route – most commonly tidal gates. At this stage you should refer to almanacs, pilot books and tidal atlases to find out how they affect matters. As more details emerge, you may find that tide times don't suit your initial plans, which were very likely determined by fundamental issues like the dates of school holidays, or your own allotted time off. Also, you may have wanted neap tides at first and discover those pencilled dates coincide with springs. There's nothing for it but to adjust the timing, perhaps putting everything back a week.

At this stage mark your tidal atlas with the relevant clock times so you know the hour in question. It's as well to realise at an early stage that HW Dover +4 is actually 0530 in the morning. As an aside, you need to be clear

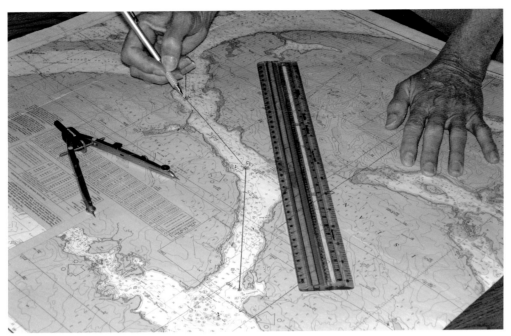

Your passage planning can start at home by plotting your intentions on a chart

about the timing convention you adopted for those on board. For most, passage planning relates to summer activities with the one hour's advance on the clock caused by BST (British Summer Time). Almost all tidal information is related to UT (Universal Time) in the UK, and of course journeys that involve a change of time zone (France etc) have a further hour to contend with. However once you're in France you might prefer local time. At the planning stage you need to decide whether you are going to work on UT, or local time, as this will have an impact (hopefully not literally) on your ability to time properly your arrival, say, at a harbour with a sill. Whatever you decide you must be consistent. So now we can go on to the next stages of our plan.

ETAs and more

Estimated times of arrival are the pivotal points around which plans revolve. By understanding them one can 'test' the plan to see if it works. A desired arrival time at the destination might mean a passage that takes much longer because of an adverse tidal flow. In which case maybe the arrival time has to be adjusted – and so the departure time may need revising. And so on.

ETAs at critical tide points

We're all familiar with the ebb and flow of tides and will know that, at certain points around the coast and at certain stages in the tidal cycle, the timing and strength of the flow can have an effect on our progress.

Common sense therefore dictates that we should try to avoid the negative effect at the tidal gate or at least time our arrival so that it ceases being a hindrance and the tide turns in our favour.

Put simply, if we're making an eastward passage through a tidal gate that flows east to west, we hope to time our arrival so:

- We arrive at one of the slack waters for a narrow gate, or…
- We arrive at the slack water at the start of the flow going in our intended direction. This latter is in the case of a tract of water that may take longer than the period of slack to transit, as slack waters tend not to last too long.

To establish these all-important facts you should refer to tidal atlases, the relevant tidal section in almanacs, or the tidal diamonds on charts. Tidal information for well-known tidal gates often appear in pilot books.

A very famous tidal gate is the area to the south of Portland Bill on England's south coast. For a westward passage one needs to round 'the Bill' between one hour before, and two hours after, HW Dover. Eastbound you should transit between five hours after, and four hours before HW Dover. As the tides can run in excess of six knots, to do anything else, except in a fast motor boat, can involve staring at the same lump of land for hours, possibly in very uncomfortable conditions if the wind is blowing in the opposite direction to the tide.

Knowing the distance to the gate and your boat's likely speed, you can determine what time you need to get there. As part of your planning it's wise to produce a series of alternative times, suiting different weather conditions.

ETA at your destination

The next consideration is the arrival time at your intended destination. Here there are a number of issues to take into account:

Portland Race: not a place to be caught with the tide against you – especially in bad weather

- Do you want your passage to be done within daylight hours or are you comfortable with a night time arrival?
- Are you familiar with the destination, lights, marks, hazards, traffic, and pilotage?
- Will the state of the tide on your arrival leave you with enough water to enter the port or anchorage?

Making a landfall, especially a new one, is very satisfying but requires care. Daylight arrivals are preferred by most, since there's usually less uncertainty. Everything seems worse in the dark. However, some skippers prefer night arrivals because, armed with a sequential list of lights and bearings, they can very quickly identify their intended route into port.

There are practical considerations too:
- A run ashore may be demanded by an eager crew or...
- ... the requirement might be just some food, and a good night's sleep.
- You may need to get to the shops before they shut.
- In popular areas marina spaces and anchorages fill up fast. To make sure of a berth it pays to arrive early.

Traffic at critical points

You will need to think about maritime traffic hot-spots along your route, including:
- Shipping entering or leaving ports and harbours, or converging on headlands.
- Shipping lanes and traffic separation schemes (TSS) which you must plan to cross at right angles.
- Military zones where warships may be exercising.

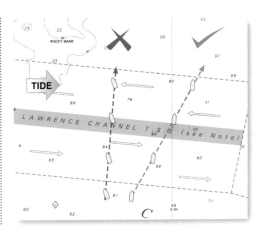

Don't attempt to stem the tide when crossing a TSS. Set a course directly across it

Hazards en route

Marine hazards are well documented. They are not always visible, and are often marked with some kind of buoyage. They fall into several groups:
- The first group consists of potential hazards that are always present, and are the obvious first consideration when drawing those first tentative lines on your planning chart. When planning your route, double check on a larger scale chart that there are no further hazards that don't appear on your planning chart.
- Then there are hazards that 'come and go' with the tide and also, sometimes, the weather. Rocks may or may not be visible, according to the state of the tide; headlands that you can pass close to at HW, but may reveal a plateau of rocks nearer low water. Always be cautious and plan for a significant safety margin. It's often simpler and less stressful to opt for deeper water and calmer seas when conditions allow.

- Tidal races also can be hazards, and should be considered as a separate issue whether they are gates or not. Whilst a following sea may be useful for a speedy passage, the conditions in the race may be too tough for your crew or boat.
- There are some broad geographic areas that themselves present hazards. For example, gunnery ranges or regions known for piracy.
- Whilst strictly speaking not hazards, many places were charted long before the advent of modern, position fixing devices, and it may be that an island that you expect to clear actually appears right on your bow! Quite serious cartographic errors can occur, even in popular areas.

TIP   **The rule is to know where your hazards are, and plan them in. Nobody likes nasty surprises.**

Day/night factors

It's a matter of broad principle that most passages will be undertaken during daylight hours, only the more extended ones are likely to involve an element of darkness. Under these circumstances perhaps the most likely scenario is a dawn departure to give a daylight arrival.

However, it should be remembered that even a day trip could involve returning in the hours of darkness, perhaps after a barbecue on the beach, and so the considerations that darkness brings become relevant. For the mariner the paradox is that darkness brings the inability to see much of what we are used to, but it does introduce new navigational

aids – namely, lights. By understanding and being aware of lit navigational marks a return passage involves 'buoy hopping' from mark to mark. Similarly any arrival at a new or familiar port can be made easy by the understanding of the routes that the lights mark, or indicate.

In its simplest form (a pilotage plan) your passage plan will make a note of the sequence of buoys and light characteristics which could be followed – perhaps simply on a scrap of paper.

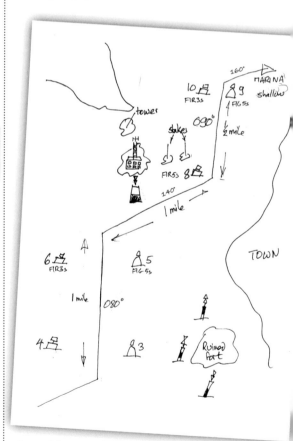

A surprising amount of information can be included in a simple sketch

You may have to wait for a lock or bridge to open

Expected conditions at arrival

The most obvious factor is the state of tide and the effect it has on landfalls, approaches and entries. Many, but not all, ports are accessible 24 hours a day. Those that aren't have to be treated carefully. If, say, a lock is only open for two hours either side of HW it's undesirable to arrive at a time outside this window, unless you can take advantage of a local anchorage or waiting pontoon to wait for the tide.

The eight key considerations

To summarise: there are eight key areas that will shape your decisions. These are:

1. **The route**
2. **Hazards**
3. **Tidal influences**
4. **Timing**
5. **Go/no go decisions**
6. **Ports en route**
7. **Landfalls**
8. **Pilotage**

For each you will need a level of detail that will be appropriate to the nature of the passage, with a proportionate amount of time spent in research and the preparation of lists, checklists, rough sketches or any other form of information to refer to.

TWG – the cornerstones of passage planning

Tides
Weather
Geography

These three elements form the foundations of passage planning. All journeys – even the simplest – call for an understanding of their influences. From here on we will be referring to TWG repeatedly.

3 PUTTING IT INTO PRACTICE

Passage A: A short inshore trip

The type of passage is often limited by the type of boat you own. For example, the owner of an open motorboat is unlikely to be planning the sort of voyages a long distance cruising yacht might be considering. Although not always the case, it's generally true that larger boats have the greater voyaging potential and have probably been purchased for that purpose.

But, whereas the scope of a passage might vary, the principles of planning it remain the same. Let's look at how various crews might assess their options and how their subsequent trip might unfold.

Our first example is a 23ft, outboard motor powered open RIB.

BACKGROUND: *Wet and Wild* isn't James and Kelly's consuming passion. They use it when the weather is right, and their hectic life permits. They tow the boat to the south coast from London – usually to Chichester or the Hamble, and occasionally to Poole. Wherever they go, they launch their boat and motor along the coast, often accompanied by their two best friends, Dave and Lizzie. They wait for relatively calm conditions when the boat can really fly, often beaching the boat or anchoring for lunch. They typically return in late afternoon or early evening, though sometimes they may stay late, having a barbecue ashore.

OBJECTIVES: Simply to have fun, enjoying the exhilarating ride, to go somewhere different from their starting point, to be able to go ashore, normally, not always, to return the same day.

CONSTRAINTS:

- If it's raining, they won't go. If the wind is fresh, and the sea a little rough, they could also cancel the trip. After all, the boat prefers calmer water, and there's no point in getting shaken to bits.
- They are a little uncomfortable with boating at night, but do have a GPS chart plotter.
- They need to have somewhere where they can anchor, or run up on the beach and go ashore with relative ease.

PLANNING CONSIDERATIONS:

- James and Kelly will need to know whether the weather will allow them to make their passage or not.
- They will need to have an idea of where they're going, which will have been obtained either by looking at the chart, reading some guide, or from prior experience.
- They must make themselves aware of any hazards en route, and ensure that they have sufficient fuel.
- With such a high speed craft, they're not very concerned about tides (although wind over tide is a factor), but must still know

about any overfalls or obstructions that may be revealed by the tide. They also need to know whether they are able to anchor in their chosen spot.

DEPARTURE: Their intended passage on the Saturday of a Bank Holiday weekend is to launch in Chichester harbour and to go a little west to Yarmouth. They will then go on to Studland the next day if the weather is kind. For them weather is the biggest TWG factor.

The weather forecast gives a south-west F3, and they will know that the tide will produce overfalls off the spit at the western end of the Solent, possibly at Christchurch Ledge, and Old Harry Rocks. The weather has been settled for some time, and so there won't be much of a sea, and their anchorage will be quiet. As they aren't constrained by tide, and they know that they can launch once they get to the coast, they have filled the fuel tank and will have a good passage round to Yarmouth.

There's nothing in the forecast to suggest any change in the weather in the next 24 to 48 hours, and so they're quite comfortable with their plans. They will have noted high water times, and have told Kelly's parents where they are going. They will have a thoroughly enjoyable day.

THEIR PLAN: James and Kelly's plan is to launch around midday at the slipway on Hayling Island, then go to Yarmouth on the Isle of Wight. After staying overnight in a B&B, they will carry on the next day to Studland at the entrance to Poole Harbour. The weather promises a continuation of the settled spell caused by a high pressure system that has been stationary for a day or two. Whilst the passage is quite a long one, they expect the sea to be calm, only disturbed by the wakes of ferries and the countless other boats enjoying this glorious weekend. They are very familiar with the density of the traffic around

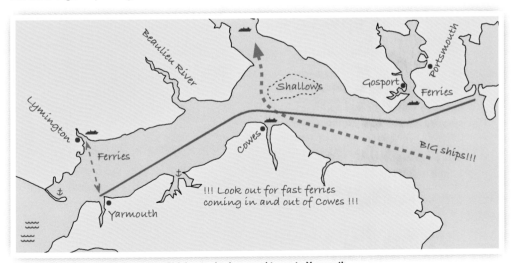

James and Kelly's plan to launch in Chichester harbour and to go to Yarmouth

Portsmouth and Southampton, and know of the moving exclusion zones established around large ships entering Southampton Water. They have not been as far west as Yarmouth before.

3	0233	1.1
	0910	4.3
Sa	1451	0.9
	2141	6.6

The tides on this beautiful spring day are giving a high water around nine o'clock in the morning. Which means that if they launch mid morning the streams in the Solent will be going westward, and they do not have to worry too much about going close inshore, or the sandbanks.

James and Kelly make their passage notes on index cards, and their plan for the passage might look something like the above.

Of course, when they put their plan into action the notes will serve only as provisional

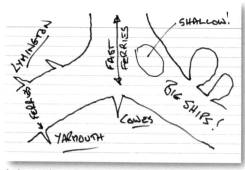

Index cards are handy for making rough notes

guides as they will go where whim dictates and according to what they see and experience. They may even decide to go into Lymington and, although not familiar with it, they will be able to find it easily and follow the well marked channel into port.

Yarmouth to Studland

The following day, James and Kelly decide they would go on to Studland. Here is their plan:

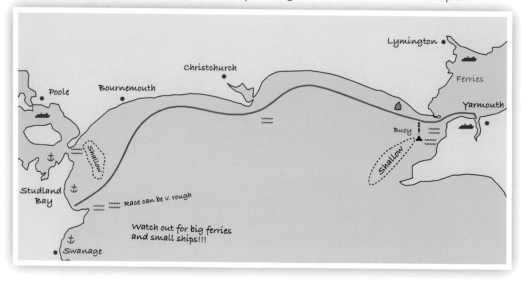

Studland Bay, Dorset – James and Kelly's final destination

In this instance, the TWG considerations are slightly different. The direct course from the western end of the Isle of Wight takes them some distance offshore. They know that the tide will be against them on the passage to Dorset and debate whether they should go out via the Needles or hug the coast once through Hurst Narrows.

They decide on the north-west passage, thereby avoiding the turbulent and crowded waters off the Needles, and also to be nearer to safety in case anything goes wrong.

Because they are coast hopping, arguably navigation isn't an issue and they are confident they will be able to locate Studland Bay just to the west of the entrance to the dredged channel into Poole.

Their passage notes for this journey could look something like this:

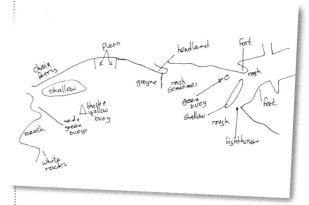

They will produce a similar one for the return journey.

Passage B:
A typical coastal passage

This involves a modest sailing vessel, countless examples of which are to be found cruising along our coasts in the summer months.

BACKGROUND: Walter and Joan have had *Delphine*, their 26 foot bilge keeler, for over 20 years. They have often thought of trading up to a larger boat, but prefer to stick with something they are very familiar with. Every weekend they make some small passage or other and, once a year, they may cruise more extensively, usually up to the west coast of Scotland from their home base in North Wales. This time they want to head across to Ireland and to cruise southwards along its east coast.

OBJECTIVES: Having made their crossing across the Irish Sea, they intend short day-sailing hops, making leisurely progress south for a week or so before heading back to North Wales. They aren't pressed to cover large mileages; rather, they want to sail gently from port to port. Ideally, each passage would not be much longer than six or seven hours. They are equally at ease at anchor or in the marina, and their boat can take the ground if need be.

Currently in Howth their intention is to do the 30 miles southwards towards Wicklow.

CONSTRAINTS:

■ Although there's only one port of refuge in this six-hour passage, unless a really nasty easterly gale sets up they are quite

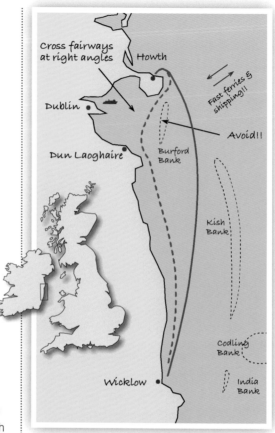

Howth to Wicklow – along Ireland's east coast

comfortable with the prospect of this passage.

■ However, they are aware that the tide runs north-south along the coast and will endeavour to avoid a wind over tide situation, and take advantage of the tidal flow.

■ If they made really good progress, they may elect to do a further 10 or so miles to Arklow. Both Wicklow and Arklow are deepwater ports which can be entered around the clock.

PLANNING CONSIDERATIONS:

- When they set sail out from Howth the demands of the passage will be fairly modest, with not much there to concern them.

- The east coast of Ireland has a series of banks running north-south, the most famous of which is the Arklow bank. If they're beating against a southerly and proceeding according to plan they will be mindful of this hazard, and will constrain their tacks accordingly.

- Their alternatives are few within the first hour. They are able to go into Dun Laoghaire, or return. Failing that there are no refuges before Wicklow.

THEIR PLAN: This will have involved noting the changes in tidal direction, and heights of tide at Wicklow, Arklow, and Dun Laoghaire, and being certain, as far as they can be, of the weather for the next 12 hours.

30 0151 1.1
0833 3.9
Mo 1429 0.9
2108 3.8

They will have made sure that they have enough food and water. They will also have assembled pilotage information for both Wicklow and Arklow, recorded all the relevant waypoints and made rough sketches of the entrances to both harbours. The local currents setting across Arklow's entrance will have been noted, as will the VHF channels used by both harbours and local sailing clubs. Since both ports are commercial, they will recognise the need to keep a lookout for traffic entering and leaving.

An alternative destination is a small drying harbour, called Courtown, even further south – a place they have always wanted to visit. But this would mean leaving much earlier if they were to arrive in daylight and with sufficient rise of tide. All in all, it seemed unlikely.

There are many 'pro formas' available. You can develop your own, or you might like to try one I favour, found in the Appendix on page 60.

Departure

Unless they have a wind over tide situation they will time their departure to arrive late afternoon/early evening, giving them time to prepare for the trip thoroughly. If the weather forecast is such that they think they might make Arklow, then they will plan to leave a little earlier than if they were just going to Wicklow. On this day the tide goes south around HW Dublin, so they aim to leave Howth at 0830, into the last vestiges of the northbound current so they get the full benefit of the southbound tidal flow later. This lift will have them arrive around 1400 to 1500, where it is just past low water and rising. Perfect.

Monitoring

It's rare for a sailing boat to follow the line on the chart. Motor boats can, and usually do, to a much greater extent. But, regardless of the type of craft, you should always have an idea how you are doing against the plan. You not only need to know how far you are to the left and right of your intended track, but you also need to know whether you are ahead, or behind in terms of distance and time. You need this information on a regular basis, so that you can have an early warning whether a Plan B might be necessary.

How often you check on progress is up to

you, as is how you do it. If, say, you want to get to a dive site at slack water your GPS will tell you how far, and how long to go. If you are on a more extended passage, regular position fixing on a chart of some sort is essential, and there is nothing more comforting than an Estimated Position or fix marked on your chart that shows you are close to your plan.

You should be comfortable with the frequency of your monitoring activities. A coastal passage in a small craft might call for half-hourly checks, a passage of 60 miles or so may call for hourly checks, and longer passages well clear of land may only need a daily position record.

Don't hide from an unpalatable truth. If things begin to look a bit awry, at the very least make the decision not to do anything about it just yet, but do conclude something. Start to think about what needs to be done when you do decide action is necessary, and dig out Plan B. Have a look at the chart. Get the latest weather forecast. Start to measure a few distances. During the voyage you must recognise that the need to change the plan might be jumping up

and down in front of you, and that you have enough information to be able to continue the voyage in safety, but to a different plan. Don't doggedly stick to your original plan. Remember that it's a live thing, and must be flexible.

Decision time!

It's important to note various points along your route when you may have to make a decision. One of the most obvious points is the famous 'point of no return'. Whilst this was most relevant for aviators, it's also appropriate in open sea passage planning. In most cases, this will be halfway along the route but, in fact, it's more complicated than this. Such influences as weather can have an impact. For instance, a following wind or sea could make the point of no return early in the passage, as the time taken to return will be longer than the outbound leg. Similarly, the behaviour of the tide at alternative ports could mean that the point of no return has to take into account the unavailability of ports of refuge along the distance of the route, or when getting to an alternative becomes impossible. The whole

Execution of a plan

Your plan is a live thing – meant to be modified and changed. There are many things that you might discover or experience that might tempt you to change your mind. Always have a 'Plan B' and even a 'Plan C'.
Let's suppose you have had a nice gentle passage to a port, but you are arriving late because the breeze was lighter than expected and had meant a slower passage. The port has a sill and you can no longer get in, but there's a peaceful cove nearby. No problem. Check the state of the tide and settle in for an undisturbed and safe night.

Nothing is cast in stone

An expression that has resonance with many is 'data rich, information poor'. It is possible to begin to plan a structure that has got so much information, so many alternatives, and so much data that it becomes counterproductive. Part of this process, as we develop the case examples, will promote the theory that you only need what you need, and anything else is superfluous. One important thing is to have the information on all means of accessing information readily available. This allows you to modify your plan 'on the hoof', and manufacture a new one, based on what changed information you think is relevant.

thing becomes even more complicated when you combine the preceding two scenarios.

Electronic versus paper charts

The rapid acceptance of electronic charting has led to questions surrounding the safety implications of relying on electronics – the marine environment plays havoc with all equipment and with none more so than electronics.

The safety case for maintaining the traditional backup is well accepted, however the rapid increase of some forms of boating has unfortunately encouraged an almost total dependence on electronic charting. Whether this is thought to be safe or not is almost immaterial, for this group of craft would certainly not have carried paper charts at all.

Increasingly the regulatory authorities are coming to conclude that electronic navigation has a place in modern day boating, and we have to accept that electronic charting is now an integral part of recreational boating.

Whatever your views on charting whilst at sea it can be argued paper charts are more appropriate for passage planning. There is the ability to see a bigger picture that's more user friendly than view-swapping on a screen, and however modern your outlook poring over a chart with pencil and ruler is a pleasurable activity.

Once you have an idea of the plan, then the notion can be incorporated into a laptop, or put on a card for transfer to the plotter.

Updating the weather

Weather information gets progressively more useless the older it gets. Knowing the anticipated weather is essential if you are to make informed decisions. This means you should get updates as frequently as you are able. This may not be so important in settled weather, but even settled weather produces hazards – fog for example.

Fortunately, modern communications mean the information is readily available. A comprehensive list of handy sources can be found in the Appendix.

Passage C: A typical short cross-Channel passage

75% of all moorings in the UK are along the south coast, and for the many people who keep their boats there, a very common passage is to cross the Channel to France or the Channel Islands. We are going to use TWG to consider a 35ft semi-displacement motor cruiser called *Happy Daze Too*.

BACKGROUND: James and Susan had to give up sailing due to advancing arthritis. Reluctant to give up their hobby altogether, they bought a 35ft twin-screw motor cruiser built along traditional lines. She is capable of more than 20 knots, but cruises more comfortably at 15 or 16. The boat is seakindly and powerful, but has to be driven at reduced speeds in a seaway because the ride begins to get uncomfortable. Based in Lymington, they are frequent visitors to the northern French coast, and in ideal conditions will go to Cherbourg for a weekend, or use it as a starting point for a North Brittany cruise, possibly by way of the Channel Islands.

OBJECTIVES: They want to start their holidays, but are undecided whether they go to Cherbourg and then south to St. Malo, or to the Channel Islands and on to North Brittany. The only real objective is to commence the holiday, so their alternatives are numerous.

CONSTRAINTS:
- They prefer not to passage-make in the open sea in winds greater than F4, actually preferring a lot less.

- They won't leave without studying the weather, watching the systems as they form and trying to work out if the current settled weather is likely to disperse as the high-pressure over north-west France dissipates. As the weather has been settled for some time, they know that the sea will be slight, but are looking at a low pressure system, tracking north-east.

PLANNING CONSIDERATIONS:
- Once they have left Lymington and are out past the Isle of Wight the options are many, and each will have been planned.
- Cherbourg and Guernsey are all-weather ports, and they do have the option of going to Poole if the idea of six hours across the channel loses its attraction. The distance travelled is not material – at least they are in another place.
- Hazards en route. They are aware of the traffic separation schemes which are marked on the charts.
- They are familiar with the east-west tidal flow, particularly on the French side of the Channel; also the huge tidal ranges that are experienced there.
- Working on a number of different departure times, they will have worked out their expected track, and aim to make sure they arrive up-tide of Cherbourg, if that is their destination. This is not strictly necessary, with a boat of *Happy Daze Too*'s capabilities, but is a legacy from their sailing days, when it was essential.
- They will choose a daylight passage, and have recorded the waypoints and other

entrance information some time ago in a format that is little more than a few notes.

- They have ensured they have full tanks and know that they have more than enough fuel for anything they might need to do, including a major diversion if necessary.

Departure

Their departure time isn't critical in such settled conditions. Had there been the remnants of a sea running they might have made sure that they passed the Needles at Bridge buoy when the currents were not meeting the swell, for this is a notorious place. They have notes of all expected weather broadcasts and will inform the UK Coastguard of their departure and intended arrival.

The same passage, but much slower

BACKGROUND: Before they gave up sailing and took up motor boating James and Susan were still regular visitors to the Channel Islands and France. However, the passage that takes them only a few hours in *Happy Daze Too* would have taken them around 12 hours in their sailing yacht. Because their yacht was only capable of about a quarter of the speed, some of the considerations they now ignore were very important indeed, and so although the journey is the same practically everything else is different. Let us look at passage planning as it might have been then, in their yacht *Happy Daze*.

OBJECTIVES: They want to start their holidays, but navigational and timing issues

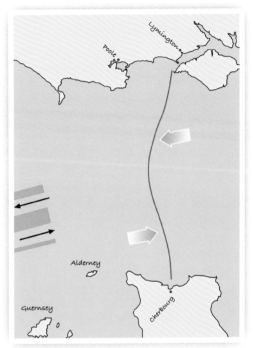

On a cross-Channel passage, the ebb tide will push you to the west and the flood tide will tend to push you back eastward again. On a 12 hour trip – typical for sailing yachts – they more or less compensate for each other

mean that they have to be sure where they intend to end up. The speed of *Happy Daze Too* means that the actual destination is immaterial, because any diversion or change of track doesn't make much difference in terms of time. As the tide runs quite strongly across the northern French coastline not only do they need to be sure of the port of arrival but need to arrive a few miles uptide of their destination so they are not swept past it and then have to fight the tide to get in. While sailing is fun they do not want to be spending hours unnecessarily at sea.

CONSTRAINTS:

- In complete contrast to preferring lighter winds, they would have been begging for winds around F4 or even greater had it been on the beam. They will still study the weather, but they will be looking for what frontal systems will bring for them in terms of wind strength and direction, and will plan a journey accordingly.

- For example, if they had intended to start their holiday in the Channel Islands and they had expected the wind to be a little north of west, and later found it was going to back, they would probably elect to go to Cherbourg. The reason for this is that they would have a passage with the wind much freer, avoiding the labour of being hard on the wind.

- If the weather had been settled for some time, they knew that the sea would have been slight with precious little wind and they would have been glumly contemplating 12 hours under engine.

PLANNING CONSIDERATIONS: The most important thing they need to know is the course they have to steer once they leave the Needles and head south.

- Their 12 hour passage will mean they have two cycles of the tide to experience, one sweeping them one way, the next sweeping them the other. Whilst you might think that these two cancel each other out (and they very nearly do) there's still the need to ensure an uptide arrival.

- If tacking is involved in this passage, they will want to make sure that they can 'lee-bow' the tide to take advantage of its lift. The nearly southerly course means that they are likely to be crossing the TSS if there is one at right angles (as they are recommended to do) but again if they're hard on the wind they may need to make some adjustments to the track to ensure they abide by these recommendations.

Departure

When they were planning their holiday they would have considered a number of departure days and times in order to take advantage of the tide. Cherbourg is a major deepwater port with access 24 hours a day – unlike many other ports in the area which are inaccessible at low tide. The normal departure from Lymington would be via the Needles, but had there been the remnants of a big sea running they might have made sure that they passed the Needles at Bridge buoy when the streams were not opposing the swell, for this is a notorious place. Under those adverse circumstances, they might choose instead to go round North Head buoy, as a less tumultuous route. They have noted times of all expected weather broadcasts and will inform the Coastguard of their departure and intended arrival.

GPS waypoints

With so many boats using GPS technology to plan and execute their routes there's a new hazard – waypoint congestion. The odds are that many mariners will adopt closely proximate waypoints with the high possibility that vessels could converge on the same bit of ocean. This isn't often a big hazard but be aware of it as you approach your waypoints, especially in bad weather or poor visibility.

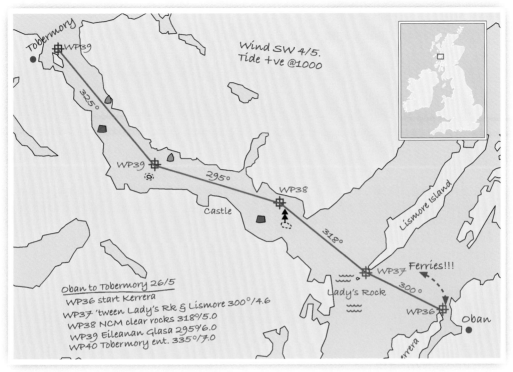

Wind SW 4/5.
Tide +ve @1000

Oban to Tobermory 26/5
WP36 start Kerrera
WP37 'tween Lady's Rk & Lismore 300°/4.6
WP38 NCM clear rocks 318°/5.0
WP39 Eileanan Glasa 295°/6.0
WP40 Tobermory ent. 335°/7.0

Oban to Tobermory – a Highlands and islands trip

Looking at the possible routes, record and enter the appropriate waypoints into your GPS. The golden rule here is double-check. Have you got the latitude and longitudes right – particularly east or west near the zero line? Confirm that the range and bearing of all waypoints from previous ones look about right, and just do a sanity check. Using no more than a pair of fingers as dividers, point to the location of the waypoints you have just entered and just see if it looks right.

The waypoints you decide to create and use should be along your intended route. Never try and modify your route to fit waypoints you may already have. A good idea is to join each waypoint with the light pencil line. Run a very brief check to make sure none of these cross headlands or run through restricted areas. Also remember that your intended track should cross traffic separation schemes at right angles, and that it should have a contingency to avoid overfalls.

And if the chart you're using in your planning is the same one that you will use to navigate, it makes sense to label the waypoints using the same convention as your GPS display. Some systems only display numbers, others will only display the first few characters of a name, so make sure the two styles marry up.

Passage D:
A typical longer passage

Longer passages tend to be undertaken by somewhat larger boats, and although there's no such thing as typical length, we're going to consider a 40ft modern sailing cruiser called *Juniper*.

BACKGROUND: *Juniper* is normally based in Brighton. Ian and Amy are both IT specialists and run a small company that can be left in the hands of their staff, though they do keep in touch via the internet. Because of their pressured lives, they enjoy spending many days at sea, and their boat is well prepared for longer distance passage making. Their

aim is to leave Brighton and sail all the way to Lorient, a passage of some 320 miles. They are both experienced sailors, and well accustomed to sailing together, but for journeys like this they take two friends with them who they have sailed with many times before. This allows them to operate a watch system that they're all familiar with.

OBJECTIVES: Their objective is to get to Lorient as, ultimately, they want to cross Biscay. They know this may not be the best of places to start from, but their daughter lives there and they want to see her and her family. Although they plan to do the whole journey in one leg, they accept that the weather could influence their activities.

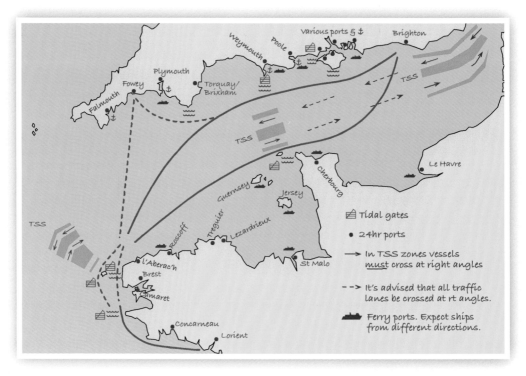

CONSTRAINTS:

There are few constraints for this foursome.

- They probably would not set out in more than F6, and would seek shelter if a gale were forecast, but apart from that they have the luxury of being confident in their own and their boat's abilities.
- Aware that a westerly would have them tacking down the Channel, they plan their route so as to minimise crossing the traffic separation schemes and shipping lanes.

PLANNING CONSIDERATIONS:

- Every port along the Channel represents a bolthole if the weather gets rough.
- They have every almanac, pilot guide and chart that's appropriate, and the onboard computer can instantly tell them when the tidal gates are and other relevant information.
- Short term planning will depend on the strength and direction of the wind. If it's in the north, south or east, they will run westwards on either the north or the south coast of the Channel.
- They will, however, be looking at the long-range forecast for they have to make some southings and want to take advantage of any shift. What will help them, for example, is if the wind is south-west, but scheduled to veer west, they would probably short tack along the English south coast and then take advantage of the veer to head south to Ouessant later on.

Their passage plan must be a live one, only finalised at the last minute when they know what the weather is going to do. At any

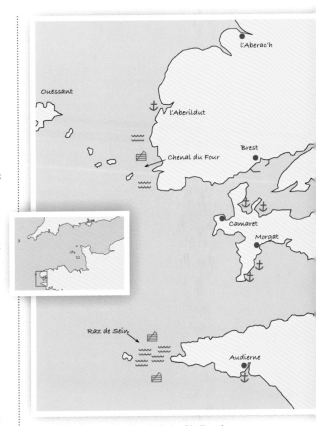

Chenal du Four to the Raz de Sein. Challenging tides make your timing crucial. Fortunately there are number of anchorages where you can wait for the right moment

stage they can seek shelter along the way. Normally, on a straight north-south passage from Falmouth through the Chenal du Four, they would try to time their arrival to take advantage of either slack water or the start of a fair tide. But in this instance accurate timing can't be guaranteed, so they could plan to go outside Ouessant, seizing the opportunity of a favourable tide for the Chenal du Four if one presents itself as they get closer.

Alternatively they could deliberately plan to end up in a port near the Chenal du Four to the Raz de Sein. Challenging tides make your timing crucial. Fortunately there are number of anchorages where you can wait for the right moment, from which they time their departure to take the Chenal du Four at the very start of the south-going flow. This would ensure their ability to carry a fair current on down and through the Raz de Sein.

The Raz de Sein is one of those stretches of water that can't be attempted in anything other than the right conditions. A sailing yacht can go through with a fair tide, but not against it. To wait at anchor within striking distance is a practical solution.

A motor boat has more chance of getting through in adverse tides and fair weather, but the ride may be pretty uncomfortable because of the seas that can arise.

Departure

Their departure time would be one that allows them to take advantage of a west-going tide

Down channel strategies

The geography and the complexity of the English Channel makes a passage from east to west an interesting navigational challenge. The fact that major shipping traffic volumes are present throughout its length, and the fact that where there are defined shipping lanes they must be crossed at right angles, means that a straightforward tacking strategy is inappropriate. The wind direction, as ever, plays a significant part. If its direction implies anything other than a windward passage the choice is simple – either to follow the UK coast or the French one. To follow the French one means a short crossing and the ability to head for the jumping off point for the southbound leg through the Chenal du Four. The traffic is generally heavier along this route but can be largely avoided by keeping closer inshore than the main traffic lanes. To follow the UK coast entails a longer crossing from a Devon or Cornish port or, if no stops are planned, to head towards north-west Brittany when appropriate. The shipping is more dispersed at this end.

The same considerations apply going to windward but quite clearly the tactics needed to make the most progress will depend on circumstances that can only be assessed with full knowledge of the weather at the time. In relative terms, short tacking along the coasts need not be short at all, and attention should be paid to the relative strengths of the tidal streams. However, most important is the ability to plan for any anticipated change to the prevailing wind so as to take the most advantage of it, and to plan to sail accordingly.

down the Channel. Since the further west they go the less significant the tides become, they would try to utilise the maximum rate for the longest time at the start of the passage, even if that meant a night-time departure.

VMG issues

All sailors are accustomed to the fact that their boat won't go directly into the wind, nor indeed into any direction within about 45° either side of the wind. Tacking to make progress towards an upwind destination lies at the very heart of sailing. If for example a destination is 10 miles upwind, and the boat can achieve five knots, we know it's going to take a great deal more than two hours to get there. Ten miles on a windward slog is probably going to take three hours, even more if the associated sea keeps knocking the speed off.

The implications of this for the passage planner are significant. If a leg of your passage is generally to windward, then the speed you plan around ought to recognise the fact that your progress towards your destination is going to be considerably slower than it would be off wind. This means that your actual progress to windward – readily found off your VMG instrument readings – needs to be monitored under way, taking advantage of any changes in wind direction that may advantage you. At the planning stage, this has to be factored in.

Of course the reverse is also true. If your destination lies off the wind and the wind changes to thwart you, your arrival time at your intended port could be considerably later. If this means missing the opening of a lock, or the tidal window during which the port is open,

you may need to plan an alternative port or prepare for a few hours at anchor somewhere.

Early passage planning might consider the implications of two boat speeds, working up two plans according to your anticipated progress. You may find that it doesn't make any difference, or you may find that an accumulation of delays at tidal gates etc may mean a rethink.

Landfalls

Whether by night or by day, a successful landfall is one of the great joys of passage making. Even if you have allowed the electronics to take care of most of the navigation, it's a good idea to confirm you are where the black box says you are by a visual fix. There are a range of techniques to confirm this, but as far as passage planning is concerned the object is to know what to expect.

Pilot books often publish silhouettes of headlands, lighthouses and any unique

coastal characteristics, and may be an essential element of your voyage to help to confirm where you are. Your passage planning might include rough sketches of distinguishing features.

Arrival in bad weather, particularly fog, is made easier by proper planning. Extra precautions might be necessary. For instance, if the port has heavy traffic, an idea of the expected arrival and departure times of the ferries will be very useful. Of course this is more difficult or even impossible with busy ports, but there's no reason why you can't contact the harbour office first or monitor the VTS to learn about port movements. Knowing the contact number or VHF channel is the crucial part of the passage planning element.

Fuel strategies

You cannot plan your fuel needs, and refuelling requirements, if you do not know how much your craft uses in various modes. You must know accurately the capacity of your fuel tank, and from that determine when you may need to refuel, if at all.

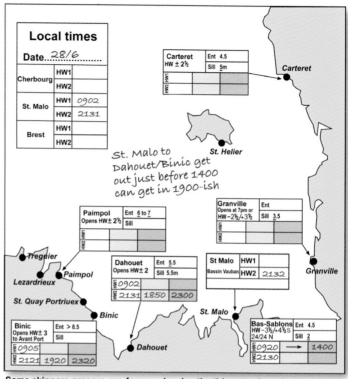

Some skippers prepare pro-formas showing the tide gates in a chosen cruising area

The golden adage for a return trip is 'one third out, one third back, and a third in reserve'. On 'A to B' passages conventional wisdom is not so specific, except that a tank should be considered empty when it has only one third of its contents left.

Almanacs and pilots list the availability of fuel in various ports. Many are open for self-service round the clock with payment by credit card, but petrol is not sold by some. Also be certain that there are no limitations on accessibility at your chosen port, for example tidal limitations.

Dirty fuel can be a real hazard, so as far as possible have a paranoid degree of cleanliness about the fuel you use, and have the necessary spares, and the tools to fit them, to allow you at the very least to change filters.

Yachts do not rely on fuel to the same extent as powered craft, perhaps using a bit at the beginning and end of each passage, but sometimes motor-sailing is a necessity, and fuel usage must be accounted for. Many boats have large ranges with a full tank, but it pays to factor in a top-up on longer passages.

TIP **Know what to expect – but don't try and make what you see fit your expectations. If it doesn't look right it probably isn't.**

Passage E: An Atlantic crossing

When international trade relied on goods being carried across oceans, the mariners of that time were pretty canny about using the elements to their advantage. It wasn't in their interests to be becalmed or thwarted by headwinds. They needed to make speedy passages and, since they were aware of the circulatory nature of the winds and currents in the world's oceans, they used them to their advantage. Nothing has changed and, in crossing oceans, the modern sailor uses the same techniques, though they are able to predict the weather in 'real time', a luxury denied to their precursors.

Although similar conditions and considerations apply to other oceans, let's take the Northern Atlantic Ocean as an example.

Figure 1 shows that its meteorology is dominated by a giant circulatory system. The high atmospheric pressure that establishes itself on top of the Azores every year provides the hub for the clockwise rotation of the prevailing winds which, in turn and because of the frictional interaction between wind and water, influence the directions of the currents. There is usually frustratingly little wind inside the Azores High itself, so mariners over the centuries have learned that the most convenient way to cross the Atlantic is to get

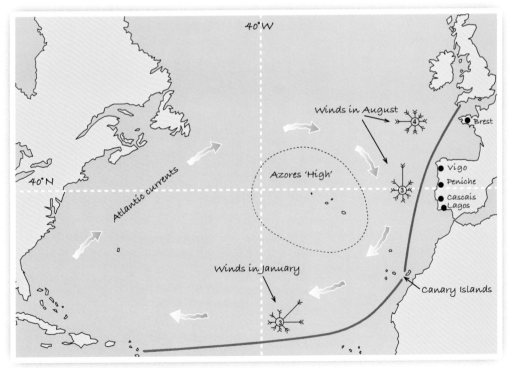

Figure 1

on to this carousel and allow it to carry you around until you reach the point where you want to get off – not the most direct route, but certainly the most practical.

Riding the carousel tends to be done in quadrants in order to take advantage of the best seasonal weather conditions throughout the passage. For an Atlantic crossing most people opt to split it up into two separate stages – the passage southwards, accomplished in the European summer months, then the westbound segment during the European winter once the hurricane season is over.

This time-honoured plan is summarised in the saying, 'head south until the butter melts and then head west'. For sailors this usually means southwards to Madeira or the Canaries where it's certainly hot enough, and then onwards to ride the favourable flows to the Caribbean. These winds, the 'Trade Winds', were the ones that facilitated trade.

Simple as that.

Timing

When it comes to planning an ocean passage, timing is everything. The hotter the oceanic region, the results of both latitude and season, the more likely it is to be subjected to dangerous tropical storms – hurricanes or cyclones depending upon local terminology. But that doesn't mean all year round. For all oceans there are months when conditions are generally benign and others that can be exceedingly dangerous. It obviously makes sense to take advantage of the former and avoid the latter.

Similarly, to head south from Northern Europe takes you across the Bay of Biscay, where the enormous depth of the ocean rises to the continental shelf, not in hundreds of gentle miles, but in a steep, short slope, a huge underwater cliff. This means that savage seas can develop in bad weather, and so is a place to avoid in winter.

By default, therefore, for a westbound Atlantic passage, the summer months are the time to head south. This could be early summer if you want to cruise France, Spain and Portugal, or later if you prefer to hurry south. Either way, you want to be in the Canaries by some time in the autumn.

So let's look at a specific example...

BACKGROUND: Pat and Jackie have been retired for several years having sold their business whilst in their mid fifties. They have been cruising more or less full-time, and have decided that having cruised the Mediterranean and northern Europe, they now want to explore some new pastures – namely the Caribbean. Their extended experience aboard means that their 50ft ketch, *Wishing*, is well prepared for long-distance sailing and carries an extensive inventory, including water makers, computers, generators, and Satcoms.

They know the boat very well indeed and have been diligent about the maintenance routines. With their considerable experience they know the value of meticulous passage planning.

THE BIGGER PICTURE: The paradox about really long passages is that the level of detail required in passage planning itself diminishes quite significantly, whilst at the same time the level of detail needed for boat preparation rises proportionately.

It is possible to argue that the only passage planning you need to do is to have a grasp of the big picture, notably the weather, most specifically wind, and currents. If we consider the popular route from the UK to the Caribbean, factors to consider are still TWG, but in the very, very broadest sense.

The normal skills and knowledge play their part, in that there are departure points, arrival points, and a lot of 'in between' but this type of planning really involves looking at the broad subject – not least the trade wind directions and the seasonal benefits and hazards.

OBJECTIVES: Their objectives for this current passage is to depart from Falmouth and head directly to Madeira, a distance of nearly 1200 NM. Their course would take them further offshore, away from the heavy traffic that streams across Biscay and around the Iberian Peninsula, a coastline they had visited in a previous cruise and were happy to miss on this occasion.

Pat and Jackie have learned that patience is one of the arts of long-distance cruising and are prepared to stay in Falmouth until the right weather presents itself. They are looking for a relatively settled weather period for the first leg and then, having got to Madeira and spent a little time exploring, they intend heading further southwards towards the Canaries where they will prepare for the Atlantic crossing.

CONSTRAINTS:

- Knowing that their time at sea means that weather systems can come and go, and having picked the time of year that is normally most favourable for a west-going passage, the only real constraint is that they won't want to start a passage knowing that there's a likelihood of persistent adverse weather.

- They are comfortable with the fact that once en route they may encounter conditions they would rather not face, but feel they have sufficient knowledge and experience and that the boat is properly equipped.

- Once en route the constraints will be those of avoiding unfavourable weather systems.

Choose the safe season

Extremely dangerous tropical storms are a seasonal menace in the lower latitudes, and prudent sailors will avoid those times when they are prevalent.

The safe time to cross the North Atlantic is during the UK's winter months when conditions are generally benign. Some time between the end of November and late May is considered ideal.

PLANNING CONSIDERATIONS:

- This is not a cruise but a voyage. Each leg will be treated as a direct passage.
- Their first leg to Madeira is treated in isolation. The second leg to the Canaries and the third to the West Indies likewise.
- Once they have left the proximity of the southern UK, alternative ports have become almost an irrelevance as the best place to go to will be the one most appropriate at the time, all other things being equal.
- Unlike a coastal passage where a number of ports of refuge may be within close reach, once under way there is nowhere very near. However, should an emergency force them to head for land, they have all the necessary charts and pilots.
- Having reached Madeira then sailed onwards to the Canaries, their route and timing across the Atlantic will generally accord with the recommendations in such guides such as the *Atlantic Pilot Atlas, Ocean Passages for the World, World Cruising Routes* and the *Atlantic Crossing Guide*. And of course they will be monitoring the weather systems by the various means available.

Departure (1)

The departure from Falmouth will be a straightforward decision: namely when favourable weather systems are predicted. August is the likely month, when the predominance of winds would be likely to give them a reasonably free sail.

The question might be asked why Pat and Jackie didn't go via the Azores – by far the shortest route to the Caribbean. The answer lies in the data panel below. A passage to the Azores involves a good deal of beating (let alone the light winds and calms that can be expected as you sail into the high) while the route to Madeira promises either reaching or – even better – broad reaching. This implies when there is a wind it is forward of the beam.

A passage to the Azores

Month	Beating (app wind 0° to 45°)	Reaching (app wind 45° to 112.5°)	Broad reaching (app wind 112.6° to157.5°)	Running
May	93% at 15.8kts	7% at 13.3kts	0%	0%
June	49% at 12.9kts	51% at 12.3kts	0%	0%
July	41% at 13.5kts	50% at 11.4kts	10% at 10kts	0%
August	61% at 13.6kts	39% at 12.3kts	0%	0%
September	84% at 14.8kts	16% at 14.9kts	0%	0%
October	94% at 17.7kts	6% at 19kts	0%	0%

However for a route to Madeira we get…

Month	Beating (app wind 0° to 45°)	Reaching (app wind 45° to 112.5°)	Broad reaching (app wind 112.6° to157.5°)	Running
May	0%	72% at 12.6kts	28% at 11.9kts	0%
June	0%	47% at 10.9kts	53% at 12.0kts	0%
July	0%	48% at 10.9kts	52% at 11.9kts	0%
August	0%	50% at 11.6kts	48% at 11.4kts	2% at 11.8kts
September	0%	45% at 12.6kts	55% at 11.2kts	0%
October	9% at 15.5 kts	40% at 16.2kts	52% at 13.1kts	0%

Departure (2)

They have been tempted to join the Atlantic Rally for Cruisers for their crossing, giving as it does a sense of companionship and security. However their experience and research leads them to conclude that, whilst Christmas in the Caribbean is attractive, and novel, they would prefer to arrive in January, when hurricanes are almost unheard of. Their passage will take a little over three weeks to complete the two and a half thousand miles, so they go back to the UK for Christmas and New Year, and set off during the first week in January.

Either way, they leave their jumping off point with expectations of a good crossing.

When you travel abroad TWG becomes TWG and O. 'O' stands for officialdom, and like all preparation, this had better be good. You are a long way from the homogenised EU, and making a landfall on the other side of the Atlantic will bring you into contact with officialdom and bureaucracy on a different scale. Be sure of the formalities you may encounter (there are plenty of insights available on the internet bulletin boards, forums, and chat rooms). Get the Visas. Be aware of currency issues. Know prohibited items. Understand local customs and ways that may seem strange, the amount of time things can take, and what sort of 'gesture' eases the way.

Your first aid kit will need attention. For some time you will have to be very self sufficient. Plan the sort of medication and self-help equipment you may need. You may have to be a dentist, nurse, or even surgeon, so seek advice, and get what you need. Remember that some drugs may be restricted in the UK, so speak with the UK authorities about having them held until departure.

Other types of craft – SOLAS still applies

To make the examples complete, and to show the importance of planning in every form of boating, let's consider a typical sea angling boat, and a typical club diving boat. Even though the launch and subsequent activity is routine, and even though divers and sea anglers go diving and sea angling, and don't consider themselves generally as boaters they must still do some passage planning, firstly to stay within the law, and secondly because it makes sense. TWG applies in every case.

1. A day sea angling

BACKGROUND: Kevin and Paul have 50-50 shares in a traditional type power boat about 7 metres in length which they keep on a swinging mooring in Plymouth. The hull is in solid GRP, there's a small cabin forward, and she's powered by a reliable diesel engine. They have an outboard motor mounted on the

Plymouth Sound – a great place to fish in the right conditions

transom as a backup. Being locals, they know the waters very well, particularly where the best fishing areas are according to weather, tides and season.

OBJECTIVES: Their objectives are to leave Plymouth, motor around Hilsea and Stoke points, and fish relatively close inshore towards the mouth of the Erme river. Should that prove unproductive they intend moving further along the coast towards Salcombe, maybe head out to the Eddystone Lighthouse and fish around there, or even try one of the well-known wrecks that abound along that coastline.

CONSTRAINTS:

- Fishing in a small boat in any kind of seaway is uncomfortable and so, given the wonderful area of protected water within Plymouth Sound, they are quite content to spend a day in its shelter should they need to.

PLANNING CONSIDERATIONS:

- They are very familiar with the tidal streams in the area and like to use them to their advantage.
- They make sure they have plenty of fuel for the engines, and for themselves in the form of sandwiches, cake and chocolate. There's a gas ring in the cuddy on which to make hot drinks.
- If they go east they are well acquainted with Salcombe and its entrance, and also know Looe and Polperro to the west. GPS points for these harbours and their favourite fishing spots, wrecks etc are stored in their plotter.

Departure

Having checked the weather they slip their moorings and go. Once they get to the breakwater though, they will reassess the situation and re-evaluate their plan.

Their plan will be most rudimentary – just a brief note – of the tidal heights, and anything in the weather forecast of note. For example, if the inshore forecast gives fair conditions, but with a deterioration 'later' they will keep an eye to the west, and be sensitive to the wind picking up. Most of the plan is in their heads.

2. A dive on a wreck

BACKGROUND: Five members of Middington Divers, a BSAC Club, intend to dive on a well known wreck near the Farne Islands. Their sport is diving and their boat a necessary accessory to it. It's a 6.5 metre RIB, powered by a 150hp outboard. It has an A-frame that carries the antennae for the GPS and radio, also a waterproof container for flares etc. Although a club boat, it is regularly maintained. They all have RYA Powerboat Level Two certificates, and are all experienced divers. They tow their RIB to the coast in the morning, hope to get two dives in each, and return in the evening.

OBJECTIVES: They all want to dive once on the wreck, with a second dive, if possible, in waters with less tidal movement.

CONSTRAINTS:

- Like any other form of boating, weather and tide constrain what they can do.
- For the wreck dive to be both safe and enjoyable, they need to be on site in the hours before and after slack water, either at high water, or low water.
- Rough waters are not conducive to good diving, mainly because of the uncertainty of keeping track of the position of those underwater, exacerbated by the uncomfortable motion of the boat.

PLANNING CONSIDERATIONS:

- They know the location of the wreck, and they have it loaded into their GPS, as well as visual points of reference.
- They also know that once a few cables out from their launch site, there are no hazards to the site, nor to the sheltered bay where they plan to do their second dive, and return.
- They know that slack water at the wreck will be about 15 minutes after high water at their corresponding standard port, and 10 minutes after low water; so they know the time they must leave to be on site at the right time to commence diving, and they also know what time the last to dive should be back on the surface.

Departure

Having got a forecast from the internet before setting off, they update it using a computer and mobile phone; and having checked the sea conditions at a headland on the way to the launch site, whether they go to dive the wreck or not is a simple decision. If they agree not to, they may then elect to dive in a more sheltered location, or not at all.

SUMMARY

Even if you have not actually completed a passage plan, however simple, or completed a passage based on your plan, by now your ability to do one is more or less complete.

This is not because you have passed some test, or done countless practice plans, but simply because you now understand, or are realising, that what is required by law, and makes good common sense, is a very simple process indeed.

TWG – tides, weather, and geography need to be understood, and the basic skills for that existed before you began to absorb all the preceding. However, whatever you are planning, or intending to plan, will involve you referring to data, whether simply local tide times, diurnal tides, or ocean circulations. To this end the following annexes and tables may be helpful. I have tried to assemble all you will find useful, but like the rest of this book it is not intended to be comprehensive, more to set you on the path of assembling your own.

You might find it helpful to photocopy the two checklists and tick off the tasks as you complete them.

BEFORE YOU START...

Collect together paper charts (even if intending to navigate electronically), publications such as pilot books and almanacs, and the navigational tools outlined on page 12. Make sure that all the data is up to date and covers your entire route and any possible deviations.

Then, for each leg of the voyage you should...

☐ Determine the straightest distance between A and B.

☐ Check the tides, noting: direction, strength, times of HW and LW and whether on Springs or Neaps.

☐ Are there any tidal constraints for any of the ports involved or any other tidal gates that might concern you? What ETAs and speeds must be achieved to satisfy tidal deadlines?

☐ Identify and make a note of any navigational hazards you might meet.

☐ Determine departure times and course to steer for each leg.

☐ Make a note of any important landmarks that will aid navigation.

☐ Make pilotage plans for departure and arrival ports.

☐ Make pilotage plans for any other ports you may have to take refuge in if the weather turns nasty or have any other urgent need to put into port. Think about how you would cope short-handed.

☐ What about your crew? Can they cope with the voyage and in what conditions? If they can't, what are their limitations?

☐ Does your crew have the necessary gear for the voyage? If not, how can they be equipped?

☐ Ask the same questions about your boat. Is it up to the voyage and, if so, in what conditions? Also does it have all the right gear?

BEFORE YOU SET OFF…

☐ Check the weather to ensure your trip remains feasible.

☐ Fill in the times in your tidal atlas and mark up the tidal curve if necessary.

☐ Enter any waypoints in the GPS.

☐ Make sure you have enough food, water, fuel, and spares on board.

☐ If going overseas ensure you have all necessary documents on board: the ship's registration papers, skipper's qualifications, and passports. And don't forget the courtesy ensign, Q flag and local currency.

☐ Brief the crew, assigning responsibility where appropriate. Set watch patterns when applicable.

☐ Log your voyage plan with the Coastguard and make sure your shore contact knows exactly what's going on.

☐ Before you cast off, recheck the latest weather bulletins and make sure your weather update equipment (NAVTEX, etc.) is configured properly.

☐ Just the final crew briefing and departure checks to go!

Bon Voyage!

ACQUIRING, ASSIMILATING AND MANAGING THE INFORMATION NEEDED

1. Communications and Recording Information

Whatever your type of passage, communications will be an issue that you need to pay heed to. There are many ways to communicate with the 'outside world' from a boat, and they vary in their effectiveness, and appropriateness. As part of the preparation for the journey you would make sure that whatever your methods and communications are to be when you are under way, you need to be certain that you are actually able to access them when you need to establish contact. A check with the marina or another boat will ensure your VHF is working properly; and even though your mobile is charged, do you have the means to recharge it?

VHF radio is the most familiar to most of us, and is the preferred method of communication with the Coastguard, and where necessary with other vessels in coastal and cross-Channel waters. Once you go further afield (or at sea) then the VHF line of sight limitations mean that other communication methods are required. The next most likely form of communication for those who make longer passages is MF radio, and increasingly satellite communications are becoming available, albeit at some considerable cost. Mobile phones are of limited use, but do have their place if you can receive a signal, and your service provider has enabled international roaming. Sometimes it is better to call the harbourmaster or a marina by mobile rather than over VHF. Whatever your sort of passage, you should not rely on mobile phones as the primary means of communication. Not only is a signal strength, or even presence an issue, but if the phone is used as a substitute for VHF there are serious safety implications that should be heeded.

A day's fishing will probably only require knowledge of today's weather, and perhaps a bit about tides – not just from where to fish, but also to be able to get back to your moorings, or to recover the boat onto the trailer. This information needs neither managing, nor any greater form of assimilation, except to be mentally aware of it. The day sail 30 miles along the coast needs a bit more information, and needs a bit of management. Longer passages require a greater degree of structure to be able to use the information properly.

How you manage the information and present it is entirely up to you and a lot depends on the way you go about things generally. A few notes scribbled on a scrap of paper may suffice. However, like so many things partly recorded and presented the information is okay under normal circumstances, but what about having to make port in deteriorating conditions with one engine out and family seasick? Preparation means that, under those pressurised circumstances, all you need is readily accessible in the format that is easy to interpret and use. Many people like to generate their own forms to fill in (and an example is included in the Appendix), so that the information you collect is presented in an easy to use, and familiar format. Once again using the TWG formula, tidal heights at the arrival port and its alternative, tidal streams during the passage, hazards en route, waypoints, times of weather forecast at destinations might be one format. Further information, like the relevant pages of an almanac or pilot, high water at Dover (or another port) for reference to tidal atlases can be added, and there may be mundane things like the telephone number of the harbourmaster at the arrival port. Whatever you do, the most important thing is to note the day, date and time of the passage.

I'm a great believer in these little forms, for they provide consistency of information. I also like the checklists for the same reason. The Appendix shows a daily form created for a cruise in Northern Brittany. Here the issue was the times that I could access ports, either over sills, or when there was sufficient rise of tide. The day's planning included working out these times and putting them into the boxes.

The key to information management is to know what information you are most likely to need and for it to be presented in a prioritised format.

Once information is recorded, it is important that you can access it. It is no use filing it away in the almanac and pilot guides, only not to be able to find it when needed. Take an entry into a rock-strewn river entrance,

one you are unfamiliar with. For your pilotage you need to know, apart from the locations of the permanently and periodically exposed outcrops, what buoys, lights and beacons are to be expected, and in what order, and at what bearing from the one you are passing, and at what distance. A diagram might be written on a sheet of paper, or card. A most useful solution adopted by racing sailors, who use it to mark the buoyage of their course, is to use a chinagraph pencil, and write the information on a bulkhead in view of the helm. Make sure it can't be rubbed off by somebody sitting there! Another method favoured by navigators is to post the information at the chart table, either using bulldog clips, tape, Blu-Tack® or other proprietary devices like Post-it® notes.

Another popular format is to use a small notebook, especially one with waterproof pages, with information for each passage on a page. When the passage is made a line is drawn through the passage plan, but not obliterating it so much that it can't be referred to for a return journey, or for the same passage on another occasion.

2. Tides

The need for tidal information is twofold. Firstly it is to know what the tidal streams are doing so that you may plan around a favourable tide, or at least minimise exposure to contrary tides; and secondly to know any limitations on your departure and arrival. The most essential point of reference is the traditional almanac. From there, you will get not only tide tables for major ports, but also information to allow you to establish tidal ranges and heights at secondary ports. They usually have a few tidal flow diagrams, and quite often some passage notes. Without doubt they are the most comprehensive source of information and constant reference will be made to them. Examples are Reeds Nautical Almanac and the splendid Bloc Marine's 'Votre livre a bord', and dedicated tidal stream atlases. These essential aids allow you to predict tidal rates and directions on an hourly basis, and can cover large areas, and some smaller specific areas like, for example, the Solent.

Tidal height information is usually published in marinas and harbour offices, and local chandleries will always have booklets containing local tides, sometimes free. Similarly yacht clubs will have reference material available to members and visitors.

Pilot guides usually have tidal stream information, usually related to a local standard port. For those who have computers on board there are countless pieces of software, either stand-alone programs, or integrated into charting software. One I am very familiar with is Neptune's Plotter Planner, which, aside from all the normal expected features, has an interface with Google Earth so you can see your planned passage, historical tracks and waypoints from space, plus a predictive animation that allows you to examine your passage into the future taking into account tides and wind. Many stand-alone plotters also have tidal information modules. For tidal information there is Belfield's Tidal Plotter, or, if you have access to the internet, tidal information is available there, especially from the UKHO's 'Easy Tide'.

3. Weather

Whether you are looking for immediate weather information connected with a passage about to take place, or you are looking for long-term information, the sources of weather are numerous. It often helps to compare several sources of information and compare them with your own interpretation. In the UK the broadcast information comes from the Meteorological Office, elsewhere from corresponding national meteorological offices. The internet, however, can give you access to weather forecasts which can be based on different prediction models, and sometimes it is interesting to compare these.

Radio broadcasts The BBC broadcasts both the shipping forecasts for the famous sea areas, and also for inshore waters around our coasts up to 12 miles offshore. The BBC also broadcasts land forecasts, and all local coastal radio stations will broadcast the weather, though the former may not necessarily be one that is much use for passage planning.

Other countries also have the national weather information broadcast on the radio and again details of these stations are available in almanacs.

VHF broadcasts The Coastguard makes regular weather forecast broadcasts six times every 24 hours and the MRCC will announce which channels to listen on, depending on your location. The information contained is the repeated or updated version of the shipping and inshore forecasts broadcast by the BBC, and there is other information, for example, about dangers to navigation, military activity, and so on. The times of the broadcasts are contained in almanacs.

Similarly in France, CROSS broadcasts are familiar, and there are parallels with English outputs, gale warnings, general situation, 24 hour forecast and trends. They also broadcast special bulletins in the event of adverse weather being anticipated. The broadcast times and the locations of the transmitters are to be found in good almanacs. If you intend to spend some time in France, it is well worth getting Meteo France's 'le guide marine'. Other countries, like Spain, Portugal, Germany and Holland also have parallel weather information services to help you.

NAVTEX One of the most useful sources of weather information, your NAVTEX is listening for weather broadcasts 24/7. Normally the information comes in a printed form, either on a screen or on paper and can be referred to after the time of receipt, or more than once. Two frequencies are used, 518kHz for the shipping forecast information and 490kHz, which tends to be of a more localised format, parallel with the inshore/offshore split in the shipping forecast. NAVTEX broadcasts can be received via dedicated NAVTEX receiver, or by a PC linked to a receiving unit. The NAVTEX receiver needs to be set up to ensure that it receives that which is wanted and rejects that which is irrelevant, particularly if the passage involves moving into a different country.

Telephone Weather can be obtained by telephone, both through commercial operations and also by talking directly to forecasters in the

Met Office. You can also call the Coastguard if you missed a forecast.

Mobile, or cell-phones The ubiquitous mobile phone is a means of getting weather information, but one of limited and unreliable use. Signal strength and availability can be more than frustrating if it leads to the loss of a crucial forecast.

HF radio facsimile broadcasts Increasingly popular, it is possible to get pictorial images of weather charts sent to your PC or dedicated receiver. Usually software is involved to interpret the broadcast and present it in a way that makes interpretation easy.

Internet The UK Met Office has a splendid site, giving everything that could possibly be needed, including satellite imagery, forecasts, gale warnings, coastal reports, animated pressure charts, and more. This information is free, but there is a further enhancement called METWeb, which can be localised to suit your requirements.

Television Increasingly TV broadcasts are no longer showing synoptic charts, and so there is little interpretation to be done from this source, but if all else fails, it is a source of information. Television weather broadcasts typically follow national and local news bulletins, and again there are equivalents in France and elsewhere.

Press The national and regional press will often feature weather forecasts, and some of them include synoptic charts.

Ask somebody There may be many occasions when you have missed the weather forecast for whatever reason, and in normal circumstances that is easy to resolve. Knowledge of the weather is an essential part of passage planning, so in order to rectify the lack of it you could ask your neighbours in the marina or anchorage. You may call a Coastguard on the telephone, but this course is not preferred, especially as they may have broadcast on VHF only a short time earlier, but they do understand the importance of knowing weather and so would be happy to give you information.

Sources of information

It is not the intention here to provide a complete bibliography of all information available for cruising. However, passage planning does involve researching and accessing sources of information for the intended passage – this point has been laboured throughout the book.

It is hoped that the following sources of information, which are grouped primarily around the concept of TWG (Tides, Weather, Geography), will be found to be of use, according to the type of passage you are intending on planning.

Many of the books themselves cover more than one aspect of TWG, especially those concerned with major ocean circulatory patterns.

Of course books aren't the only source, as much information is available on the internet.

1. Tides (and Currents)

Atlantic Pilot Atlas	J. Clarke
Atlas of Pilot Charts – North Atlantic Ocean and Caribbean	US Defence Mapping Agency
MP 203 Tide Tables – Indian Ocean and South China Sea	UKHO
MP 204 Tide Tables – Pacific Ocean	UKHO
NP 136 Ocean Passages for the World	UKHO
NP 201 Tide Tables – UK and Ireland	UKHO
NP 202 Tide Tables – Europe Mediterranean and Atlantic	UKHO
NP 209 Orkney and Shetland Islands	UKHO
NP 218 North Coast of Ireland and West Coast of Scotland	UKHO
NP 219 Portsmouth Harbour and Approaches	UKHO
NP 220 Rosyth Harbour and Approaches	UKHO
NP 221 Plymouth Harbour and Approaches	UKHO
NP 222 Firth of Clyde and Approaches	UKHO

NP 233 Dover Strait	UKHO
NP 249 Thames Estuary	UKHO
NP 250 The English Channel	UKHO
NP 251 North Sea Southern Part	UKHO
NP 252 North Sea North Western Part	UKHO
NP 253 North Sea Eastern Part	UKHO
NP 254 The West Country Falmouth to Teignmouth	UKHO
NP 255 Falmouth to Padstow including Scilly Isles	UKHO
NP 256 Irish Sea and Bristol Channel	UKHO
NP 257 Approaches to Portland	UKHO
NP 258 Bristol Channel Lundy to Avonmouth	UKHO
NP 259 Irish Sea Eastern Part	UKHO
NP 263 Lyme Bay	UKHO
NP 264 The Channel Islands and Adjacent Coasts of France	UKHO
NP 265 France West Coast	UKHO
NP 337 The Solent and Adjacent Waters	UKHO
Street's Transatlantic Crossing Guide	D. M. Street Jr
The Atlantic Crossing Guide	A. Hammick & G. McLaren
The Yachtsman's Manual Of Tides	M. Reeve-Fowkes
Tidal Current Tables Atlantic coast of North America and Asia	NOAA
Tidal Current Tables Pacific Coast of North America and Asia	NOAA
Tidal Streams Between Portland Bill and St Albans Head	P. Bruce & J. Watson
Tide Tables East Coast of North and South America	NOAA
Tide Tables Europe and West Coast of Africa	NOAA
Tide Tables West Coast of North and South America	NOAA
World Cruising Handbook	J. Cornell
World Cruising Routes	J. Cornell
Yachting Monthly's Sailing an Atlantic Circuit	A. Buchan
Yachtsman's Tidal Atlas – Channel Ports and Approaches	M. Reeve-Fowkes
Yachtsman's Tidal Atlas – Central Channel and Solent	M. Reeve-Fowkes
Yachtsman's Tidal Atlas Southern North Sea and Eastern Channel	M. Reeve-Fowkes
Yachtsman's Tidal Atlas Western Channel	M. Reeve-Fowkes

2. Ocean Weather

GMDSS Forecasts (Global Maritime Distress and Safety System)
GMDSS is an all-encompassing worldwide weather and safety system. Depending on the location, you may be able to access weather information from several sources.

VHF radio
Usually confined to coastal waters because of the physical limitations of line-of-sight transmissions, times of broadcast and areas covered are to be found in almanacs, and from the internet. Different countries have slightly different routines, but are the same in principle.

NAVTEX
Whilst cumbersome, and a little dated in appearance, the range of NAVTEX broadcasts make it a primary source of weather information, hundreds of miles out to sea. Times etc are again available from the internet, and the ubiquitous almanac.

INMARSAT-C
Beyond the range of NAVTEX, Inmarsat is the source of information for the deep-sea sailor.

RTTY
Radio teletype is disseminated through HF/SSB radio broadcasts, and is more common in the US than Europe, though the German Weather Service uses it.

Internet
There is extensive weather information on the internet, with almost nothing that cannot be found. However, you may not have access depending on your location and it can be costly when travelling overseas.

GRIB Files and Services
Gridded Information in Binary (GRIB) is a computer code developed to format weather information in a binary code so that the huge amount of data could be exchanged internationally. The files need a piece of software, readily available, to extract the data and re-present it usually but not universally in a graphical format. Depending on your requirements, they can either be free, or cost.

Maritime Mobile Radio Nets for Cruisers
These longer range SSB radio-based communities exist all over the world, on both maritime and amateur radio frequencies, and are run by volunteers for the benefit of long distance cruising sailors. They provide weather information, pass health and welfare traffic and help individual vessels pass traffic to those outside a given frequency's 'footprint'. They use the HF frequency bands.

Caribbean M/M Net	Caribbean
Chubasco Net	Mexico west coast
Coconut Breakfast Cruisers Net	Weather Marquesas, Tuamotus, Society Islands
Comedy Net	South-west Pacific
Cruiseheimer's Net	US east coast & Eastern Caribbean
European Maritime Mobile Net	
German Maritime Mobile Net	Atlantic, Pacific, Indian Ocean, Med
Herb Hilgenberg's Southbound Net	Weather forecasts for Atlantic & Caribbean
Italian M/M Net Weather	North & East Atlantic & Atlantic to Tropic of Capricorn
'Le Reseau Du Capitaine' Net	Atlantic, Caribbean & Pacific
Manana M/M Net	US west coast to Hawaii
Maritime Mobile Service Net	Atlantic, Eastern Pacific, Gulf of Mexico
Mediterranean Maritime Mobile Net	
Mississauga Maritime Net	Europe, Med, Atlantic, Caribbean and Central America
Mobile Maritime Net – South East Asia	Japan to Seychelles – Hong Kong to Northern & Western Australia
Northwest Caribbean Cruiser's Net	Mexico to San Andres Island, Colombia
Pacific Inter-Island Net	Micronesia to Hawaii
Pacific Maritime Mobile Service Net	Pacific/worldwide
Pacific Seafarers Net	Pacific
Panama Canal Connection Net	Pacific from Mexico to Galapagos, Atlantic from Belize to Colombia
PST Baja California M/M Net	Coastal Baja & California
Radio 'Peri-Peri'	Indian Ocean & S Atlantic
Robby's Net	Australia
Roy's Net	North & West Indian Ocean
Russell Radio	Bora Bora to Australia
South Africa Maritime Mobile Net	Indian Ocean & S Atlantic
Tony's Net	Indian Ocean & Red Sea
Tony's Net	South Pacific & Australia
TransAtlantic Maritime Mobile Net	Med, N & S Atlantic and Caribbean
U K M/M Net	Covers UK waters, Med & Atlantic

There are many books about the weather, but for specific passage making

Mediterranean Weather Handbook for Sailors	R. Ritossa
Modern Marine Weather	D. Birch

3. Geography

MULTI-REGION	
The Cruising Association Almanac	Cruising Association
The Reeds Nautical Almanac	Adlard Coles
The Reeds Western Almanac	Adlard Coles
The Reeds Channel Almanac	Adlard Coles

UK & IRELAND	
Bristol Channel and Severn Cruising Guide	P. Cumberlidge
Bristol Channel and Severn Pilot	P. Cumberlidge
CCC Sailing Directions: Ardnamurchan to Cape Wrath	Clyde Cruising Club
CCC Sailing Directions: Firth of Clyde inc. the Solway Firth and Isle of Man	Clyde Cruising Club
CCC Sailing Directions: Kintyre to Ardnamurchan	Clyde Cruising Club
CCC Sailing Directions: Outer Hebrides	Clyde Cruising Club
Crossing the Thames Estuary	R. Gasper
Cruising Anglesey and Adjoining Waters	R. Morris
Cruising Cork and Kerry	G. Swanson
Cruising Guide to Northwest England and Wales	G. Griffiths
East and North Coasts of Ireland	Irish Cruising Club
East and North Coasts of Ireland Sailing Directions	Irish Cruising Club
East Coast Pilot	C. Jardine, G. Cooper, & D. Holness
East Coast Rivers Cruising Companion	J. Harper
Firth of Clyde	Clyde Cruising Club
Forth Tyne Dogger Humber	H. Irving
Irish Sea pilot	D. Rainsbury
Isles of Scilly Pilot	J. & F. Garey
Lundy and Irish Sea Pilot	D. Taylor
North and North-East Coast of Scotland	Clyde Cruising Club
North Sea Passage Pilot	B. Navin
South and West Coasts of Ireland	Irish Cruising Club
South and West Coasts of Ireland Sailing Directions	Irish Cruising Club
Southern Island Cruising Companion	R. Wilcox

The Channel Cruising Companion	L. Featherstone
The Channel Islands	RCC Pilotage Foundation
The Reeds Channel Almanac	Adlard Coles
The Reeds Eastern Almanac	Adlard Coles
The Scottish Islands	H. Haswell-Smith
The Shell Channel Pilot	T. Cunliffe
The Yachtsman's Pilot to Skye and North West Scotland	M. Lawrence
The Yachtsman's Pilot to the West Coast of Scotland: Clyde to Colonsay	M. Lawrence
The Yachtsman's Pilot to the West Coast of Scotland: Crinan to Canna	M. Lawrence
The Yachtsman's Pilot to the Western Isles	M. Lawrence
UK and Ireland circumnavigated guide	S. Steel
West Country Cruising	M. Fishwick
West Country Cruising Companion	M. Fishwick
West Highland Shores	M. Drummond
MAINLAND EUROPE	
ABC Guide to Sailing the Costas	S. Cole
Adriatic Pilot	T. & D. Thompson
Atlantic Spain and Portugal	A. Hammick
Brittany and Channel Islands Cruising Guide	D. Jefferson
Cruising Galicia	C. Rojas & R. Bailey
North Biscay	G. McLaren
North Biscay	RCC Pilotage Foundation
North Brittany	RCC Pilotage Foundation
North Brittany and Channel Island Cruising Companion	P. Cumberlidge
North Brittany and Channel Islands	J. Lawson
North France and Belgium Cruising Companion	N. Featherstone
Secret Anchorages of Brittany	P. Cumberlidge
South Biscay	RCC Pilotage Foundation
South Biscay Pilot	J. Lawson

THE ATLANTIC CIRCUIT	
Around the World Cruising Guide	A. Phillips
Atlantic Crossings	L. Weatheritt
Atlantic Islands	RCC Pilotage Foundation
Canary Islands Cruising Guide	J. Cornell
Cruising Guide to West Africa	S. Jones
North Biscay	RCC Pilotage Foundation
North-West Spain Cruising Companion	J. Detlef
Ocean Passages and Landfalls	R. Heikell & A. O'Grady
South Atlantic circuit	RCC Pilotage Foundation
The Atlantic Crossing Guide	A. Hammick & G. McLaren
The Atlantic Sailor's Handbook	A. Buchan
World Cruising Handbook	J. Cornell
Your First Atlantic Crossing	L. Weatheritt

ISLANDS OF THE ATLANTIC CIRCUIT	
A Cruising Guide to the Caribbean	W. T. Stone & A. M. Hays
A Cruising Guide to the Leeward Islands	C. Doyle
A Sailor's Guide to the Windward Islands	C. Doyle
Anguilla to Dominica	D. M. Street Jr
Atlantic Islands	A. Hammick
Azores Cruising Guide	G. Cornell
Canary Islands Cruising Guide	J. Cornell
Concise Guide to Caribbean Weather	D. Jones
Cruising Guide to the Virgin Islands	N. & S. Scott
Cruising Guide to Trinidad and Tobago plus Barbados	C. Doyle
Cruising Guide to Venezuela and Bonaire	C. Doyle
Exumas: Explorer Charts	M. Lewis
Faeroe Iceland & Greenland	RCC Pilotage Foundation
Madeira and Porta Santa Cruising Guide	G. Cornell
Martinique to Trinidad	D. M. Street Jr
Passages South: A Gentleman's Guide	B. Van Sant
Puerto Rico the Passage Islands the US and British Virgin Islands	D. M. Street Jr

Reeds Nautical Almanac: Caribbean Edition	
The Bahamas Cruising Guide	M. Wilson
The Central and Southern Bahamas Guide	S. Pavlidis
The Cruising Guide to Abaco	S. Dodge
The Exuma Guide	S. Pavlidis
Venezuela	D. M. Street Jr
VIP Cruising Guide – St Maarten to Antigua	W. J. Eiman
Virgin Anchorages	N. & S. Scott
Yachting Guide to Bermuda	E. Harris
Yachtsman's Guide to the Bahamas	M. Fields
Yachtsman's Guide to the Virgin Islands	M. Fields
Yachtsman's Guide to the Windward Islands	J. M. Wilensky
US EAST COAST AND CANADA	
A Cruising Guide to New Jersey Waters	D. M. Launer
A Cruising Guide to Nova Scotia	P. Loveridge
Atlantic Coast	Embassy Marine
Chesapeake Bay Cruising Guide: Vol 1 Upper Bay	T. Neale
Coastal Guide to New England	J. P. Ware & W. Fenn
Cruising Guide to Coastal North Carolina	C. S. Young
Cruising Guide to Coastal South Carolina and Georgia	C. S. Young
Cruising Guide to Eastern Florida	C. S. Young
Cruising Guide to Maine Vol 1: Kittery to Rockland	D. Johnson
Cruising Guide to Maine Vol 2: Rockport to Eastport	D. Johnson
Cruising Guide to Narragansett Bay & the South Coast of Massachusetts	L. & P. Childress & T. Martin
Cruising Guide to the Bay of Fundy and the St John River	N. Tracy
Cruising Guide to the Florida Keys	F. Papy
Cruising Guide to the Labrador Coast	S. Weld
Cruising Guide to the Maine Coast	H. & J. Taft & C. Rindlaub
Cruising Guide to the New England Coast	R. F. Duncan
Cruising Guide to the Nova Scotia Coast	J. McKelvy
Cruising the Chesapeake: A Gunkholer's Guide	W. Shellenberger
Eldridge Tide and Pilot Book	M. Jewett White

Florida's East Coast	Embassy Marine (EMP)
Guide to Cruising the Chesapeake Bay	Chesapeake Bay Magazine
Intracoastal Waterway Facilities Guide	B. & B. Smith
Light List & Waypoint Guide: Maine to Texas	J. & L. Kettlewell
Long Island Sound	Embassy Marine
Reeds Nautical Almanac: North American East Coast	
Rhode Island Maine and New Hampshire	
The Cruising Guide to Newfoundland	S. Weld
The Intracoastal Waterway Chartbook	J. & L. Kettlewell
The Intracoastal Waterway, Norfolk to Miami	J. & B. Moeller (IM)
Waterway Guide Mid-Atlantic Edition	
Waterway Guide Northern Edition	
Waterway Guide Southern Edition	
Where the Wind Blows: Marine Weather Canada	P. J. Bowyer
Yachting Guide to the South Shore of Nova Scotia	A. M. Dechman

ENDPIECE

Some time after you put this book down, you will be intending to go to sea in a craft of some sort. You will start from some point, complete your passage, and come ashore. Prior to doing that I hope you will have planned and prepared for it, and that this book may have helped or provided the foundation for that and any subsequent voyage.

Enjoy your boating – you should be able to, for you, your family, friends or crew will be safer for the thoughts that will have been the foundation of an easy time at sea.

From	....	Date	....
To	....	Start	....
Distance	....	Wind	....
Passage time	....	Stream	....

Sea Area	Wind now	Wind later	Weather	Vis
Inshore				

Port	Tide	Time	Ht	Time	Ht
	HW				
	LW				
	Range				
	HW				
	LW				
	Range				
	HW				
	LW				
	Range				
	HW				
	LW				
	Range				
	HW				
	LW				
	Range				

Tide goes	at		from	till
Tide goes	at		from	till

A sample passage planning information form that you may wish to photocopy.

GLOSSARY

Back: Said of wind direction that changes in an anti-clockwise direction.

Beam reach: Sailing with the wind 'abeam' – i.e. coming directly from one side.

Beat: To sail as close to the wind's direction as possible. Also called 'close hauled'.

Berth: A place to moor, or for someone to sleep.

Bow: The forward part of the boat. Port and starboard bows are either side of the stem.

Broad reach: A point of sail where the wind is from aft of the beam but not directly (or nearly) astern.

Cable: Nautical measurement – a tenth of a nautical mile, about 200 yards or 185 metres.

CEVNI: Code Européen des Voies de la Navigation Intérieure. This allows the inland waters category of an ICC to be validated.

Close hauled: See 'Beat'.

Close reach: A point of sail somewhere between a beat and a beam reach.

Cockpit: The external control centre of a boat, for steering and sail trim.

Colregs: Colloquial expression for the International Regulations for the Prevention of Collision at Sea, IRPCS.

CROSS: Centre Regional Operational de Surveillance et de Sauvetage – the French Coastguard.

Day-sail: A passage usually made during a single period of daylight.

Dead reckoning: The type of navigational computation which attempts to establish a position by the course steered and distance run through the water.

Downtide, Downstream: To run in the same direction as the tide or stream.

Downwind: Sailing in the same general direction of the wind.

DSC: Digital Selective Calling. A system whereby a VHF radio transmitter can make an automatic digitised call to a selected station.

ETA: Estimated Time of Arrival.

Fairway: The main channel into the harbour. That part of an approach channel lying outside of a harbour entrance.

GMDSS: Global Maritime Distress Safety System.

GPS: Global Positioning System.

Heading: The direction in which you are sailing or would like to sail.

HF: High frequency.

ICC: International Certificate of Competence.

IRPCS: See 'Colregs'.

Knot: One nautical mile per hour. The oft-heard phrase 'knots per hour' is nonsensical since it would mean 'one nautical mile per hour per hour'.

LAT: Lowest Astronomical Tide.

Lee: The protected downwind side of an object.

Lee-bow: Sailing across a tidal stream such that the effect is to make the boat's track closer to the wind.

Lee Shore: Land that lies to 'leeward' of yourself. Not good news in heavy weather.

Leeward: The side of the boat facing away from the wind.

Marina: A sheltered area with berths and other facilities for boaters.

Met Office: The UK's Meteorological Office.

Meteo: The French Meteorological Office.

MF: Medium frequency.

MRCC: Maritime Rescue Co-ordination Centre

Neap Tides: Or simply 'neaps'. The lesser tide experienced every two weeks when the sun and moon are pulling against one another at half-moon.

Plotter: Electronic device which displays charts, and can plot GPS positions, tracks, waypoints etc.

Pointing: Sailing as close to the wind as possible. A boat that 'points high' will sail closer to the wind than one that 'points low'.

Reach: See 'Beam reach', 'Broad reach' and 'Close reach'.

Reef: To reduce sail area.

RIB: A Rigid (hulled) Inflatable Boat. Usually a small powerboat.

Running: Sailing downwind – i.e. with the wind coming from astern.

RYA: Royal Yachting Association – the sport's UK national governing body.

SAR: Search and rescue.

SatComs: Abbreviation for Satellite Communications.

Sill: A device, either fixed or movable, that contains water in a harbour.

SOLAS: The International Convention for the Safety of Life at Sea.

Stream: The flow or movement of water, whether caused by current or tide.

Tacking: The zig-zag course of a boat sailing upwind.

Tideway: Channels where the effects of tidal stream can be felt.

Uptide: Upstream, in a direction against the flow of water.

UT: Universal Time (and UTC – Coordinated Universal Time).

Veer: Said of wind direction that changes in a clockwise direction.

VHF: Very high frequency.

VMG: The speed at which a boat makes progress towards its intended destination (Velocity Made Good).

Waypoint: A nominal position on a chart.

Windward: Towards the direction from which the wind blows.

INDEX

continued overleaf